CW01678408

PENGUIN MOD

Regret

IKRAMULLAH (CHAUDHRY) was born in 1939 in Jandiala, a small village in the Nawan Shehr district of Jalandhar in India. He finished high school in Amritsar. After Partition his family moved to Multan where he did his BA in 1953 and two years later took a law degree from University Law College at Lahore. After practising law in Multan for a few years, he went into the insurance business in 1965, retiring in 1990. He has been writing fiction since 1962 and published several collections of short stories and novellas, one of which, *Gurg-e Shab* (Nocturnal Wolf), was banned soon after its publication in 1978. More recently, he has published a novel, *Saa'e ki Aavaaz* (The Shadow Speaks).

RAJA FARUQ HASSAN was born in 1939 in Lyallpur (now, Faisalabad, Pakistan) and died in 2011 in Montreal. He held degrees in English studies from the universities of Punjab, Leeds, and New Brunswick, and taught at Dawson College and McGill University, Montreal. He was a published Urdu poet, critic and translator. With Khalid Hassan he co-edited *Versions of Truth: Urdu Short Stories from Pakistan* (Vikas 1983). His last published work before his death was a book of poems by the celebrated Turkish poet Nazim Hikmat, which he translated from English.

MUHAMMAD UMAR MEMON is Professor Emeritus of Urdu literature and Islamic Studies at the University of Wisconsin-Madison. He is a critic, short-story writer, translator and the editor of *The Annual of Urdu Studies* (1993–2014). He has translated half a dozen anthologies of Urdu fictional writing. His latest published work is *The Occult* (Penguin), a translation of the critically acclaimed Urdu writer Naiyer Masud's volume of short stories, *Seemiya*.

IKRAMULLAH

Regret

TWO NOVELLAS

Translated from the Urdu by
Faruq Hassan and Muhammad Umar Memon

PENGUIN BOOKS

PENGUIN BOOKS
Published by the Penguin Group
Penguin Books India Pvt. Ltd, 7th Floor, Infinity Tower C, DLF Cyber City, Gurgaon 122 002, Haryana, India
Penguin Group (USA) Inc., 375 Hudson Street, New York, New York 10014, USA
Penguin Group (Canada), 90 Eglinton Avenue East, Suite 700, Toronto, Ontario, M4P 2Y3, Canada
Penguin Books Ltd, 80 Strand, London WC2R 0RL, England
Penguin Ireland, 25 St Stephen's Green, Dublin 2, Ireland (a division of Penguin Books Ltd)
Penguin Group (Australia), 707 Collins Street, Melbourne, Victoria 3008, Australia
Penguin Group (NZ), 67 Apollo Drive, Rosedale, Auckland 0632, New Zealand
Penguin Books (South Africa) (Pty) Ltd, Block D, Rosebank Office Park, 181 Jan Smuts Avenue, Parktown North, Johannesburg 2193, South Africa

Penguin Books Ltd, Registered Offices: 80 Strand, London WC2R 0RL, England

Regret first published in Urdu as 'Pashemaani' in *Sawa Neze par Suraj* by Sang-e-Meel, Lahore 1998
Out of Sight first published in Urdu as 'Aankh Ojhal' in *Bar-e Digar* by Fiction House, Lahore
First published by Penguin Books India 2015

10 9 8 7 6 5 4 3 2 1

ISBN 9780143423126

For sale in the Indian Subcontinent only

Typeset in Minion Pro by R. Ajith Kumar, New Delhi
Printed at Replika Press Pvt. Ltd, India

A PENGUIN RANDOM HOUSE COMPANY

Contents

Brief Introduction and Acknowledgements

Regrettably, one is both struck and baffled by the conspicuous absence of Ikramullah from contemporary Urdu critical discourse. And yet he is a major writer in Pakistan today, with a substantial body of writing: two collections of short stories, *Jangal* (Forest) and *Badalte Qaalib* (Shifting Shapes); a collection of three short stories and three novellas, *Baar-e Digar* (A Second Time); a collection of four novellas, *Sawa Neze par Suraj* (Under the Scorching Sun); a novella, *Gurg-e Shab* (Nocturnal Wolf); and, more recently, a novel, *Saa'e ki Aavaaz* (The Shadow Speaks).

This may seem meagre capital to show for over half a century of writing, but Ikramullah, though not unsociable, is nonetheless an exceptionally private person who seems to be rarely affected by the desire to conform to, or even to marginally satisfy, what the world might expect of him. He writes for himself and, as Jorge Luis Borges once remarked, 'Perhaps for a few personal friends.'[1] When Borges's first

[1] 'The Art of Fiction XXXIX: Jorge Luis Borges', *The Paris Review*, No. 40 (Winter–Spring 1967), p. 151.

book, *A Universal History of Infamy*, sold only thirty-seven copies, he wanted to find those buyers to apologize for the book and thank them. He would have been content had only seventeen—why, even only seven—copies been sold. At least those people were real. They had a face and lived each on a particular street. But the millions across the world who would read him in umpteen languages were 'too vast . . . for the imagination to grasp'.[2]

Now Borges may be exaggerating or joking (he had a great sense of humour and loved a dash of spicy jokes even in the midst of serious conversations), but there is plenty of substance in his remark, though it may puzzle our mundane sensibilities.

I mention Borges to underscore a capacity to blot out the world and concentrate on writing—a capacity found in many good writers, pre-eminently in William Faulkner, who wrote *The Sound and the Fury* five separate times but felt the book 'was still not complete . . . I couldn't leave it alone, and I never could tell it right, though I tried hard and would like to try again, though I'd probably fail again'.[3]

Ikramullah may or may not work as hard as rewriting a piece four or five times over, or be as timid as Borges, but he does share with many true writers the ability not to involve himself too much with the way business gets done in the publishing world, or care for the opinion of his reader or critic. He prefers to keep his eyes totally focused on the work, exuding a vigorous sense of autonomy, a gritty self-sufficiency.

---

[2] Ibid., pp. 125–26.

[3] 'The Art of Fiction XII: William Faulkner', *The Paris Review*, No. 12 (Spring 1956), pp. 39–40.

When Penguin asked me for a photo of the author and an endorsement to go before the blurb on the back cover to conform to the format of Penguin Modern Classics, I found myself in a fix. I couldn't find anything on Ikramullah in English except a few paragraphs by Salim-ur-Rahman on the *Badalte Qaalib* collection and a few comments of Salim Akhtar and Muhammad Khalid Akhtar in Urdu, which appeared as blurbs for the author's first collection of short stories, *Jangal,* and the novella *Gurg-e Shab*. But shouldn't I perhaps write to him for these? I was hesitant—because although he knew that Faruq Hassan and I had been translating his stories since the mid-1990s, he never evinced interest in our enterprise or asked about its progress—a sort of *be-niyaazi* he shares, in my experience, with at least one other Urdu writer, Naiyer Masud. Anyway, I overcame my diffidence and contacted him by e-mail through a friend of his. Some time later I received the following:

'Dear Mr Memon, I am not in favour of printing an author's photograph on the book. No comments of famous writers are presently available. I do not preserve such writings.'

So that was that! I felt like an intruder, but his detachment was hardly a reason to take umbrage. That I later did find a photo and an endorsement was thanks to Salim-ur-Rahman. Which, of course, does not change the fact that very little has been written about Ikramullah's work and he is the type of person who doesn't go after visibility or publicity.

The novellas *Regret* and *Out of Sight* presented here do 'skilfully evoke the long shadow cast by the violence of Partition'; however, Partition, here, exists only as a vague if pervasive presence. They evoke much more than just its effects, horrible though they were and continue to be so to this day in unexpected transmutations. Ikramullah, who needs an expansive canvas to give full rein to his tremendous narrative skills, has the rare ability to bring to life a whole period, a manner of living, by his microscopic attention to the minutest, fleeting detail. He captures the slightest vibrations of feeling and unarticulated thought with remarkable precision, while keeping himself at an emotional distance from the events. It is not just Partition, or any specific event, that may be identified as the terminal intent of either work, but rather time itself and the process by which lives unfold and individual histories are written through life's meandering course before being erased from memory as the main actors exit the scene.

We encounter 'nearly all the distinct facets of modern Urdu fiction in Ikramullah's stories', writes Salim-ur-Rahman, 'menacing cityscapes, proliferating violence, postures of despair, instances of magic realism and examples of straightforward realistic narration.'[4] But, as often, he also deals head on with taboo subjects: the plight of people who eke out a difficult life on the margins of society as they slosh through the confounding maze of their own confused impulses and ravaged psyches. In *Out of Sight* he writes about the Ahmadis, a subject that Urdu fiction has coyly bypassed, but the subtext tells a story of capitalist greed played out against the background of craftily calibrated sectarian machinations.

In an earlier novella, *Gurg-e Shab*, banned by the censor

[4] 'Double Exposure', *Friday Times* (date of publication and page number not available).

for 'obscenity', Ikramullah delves into the convoluted mindscape of an offspring of incest and the latter's desperate attempts to shake off the devastating psychological effects of his illegitimate birth—rather like Blanca Williams in Abdullah Hussein's debut short story 'Naddi' (The Brook), a child abandoned one cold morning by the side of the street—and his eventual failure. While Blanca finds peace in the cascading waters of the Niagara Falls, Zafar goes through various frightening stages of madness. The author's skilful management of shifts between third- and first-person narrators uncovers the inner workings of Zafar's troubled mind with an intensity as awesome as it is tragic. The consciousness of being a 'bastard' wrecks his life, so much so that his longing for female love is cruelly thwarted by his own inability to engage with women physically. While the centre stage is occupied by the protagonist's cerebral trauma, the narrative is as much a story of his mother who exists only on the outer fringes of the work. In a deft treatment of the ancillary subject of how young women are too often married off to old men for money or other advantage, only to remain deprived of sexual gratification and tender love, the author posits a parallel between Zafar's mother and his own lover, the stunningly beautiful Rehana.

The mother, dissatisfied with her husband, established sexual relations with her own stepson, (Zafar's older stepbrother who is actually his biological father). Likewise Rehana—the young wife yoked to the outrageously rich and atrociously revolting A.B. Shaikh—was only too willing to sleep with Zafar. When their two bodies come together, the raging conflicts in Zafar's mind take over and affect his ability to slake Rehana's thirst or his own. In a strange twist of logic—

or poetic justice—the mother's success in finding gratification apart from the marital bed dooms her own son who is unable to provide the same gratification to the woman he so desires.

In the novella *Sawa Neze par Suraj,* the author takes on another subject that has attracted scant attention in Urdu fiction: the realization of the onset of love between two males. Homosexual or gay love seems almost too loud to describe the hesitant tender feeling of mutual attraction, vague but unmistakable, that exists between the shy, delicate, youthful Chooza and his friend Boom. Too diffident to articulate, both unerringly sense something different in their relationship. The reader can only imagine how it would have turned out had Chooza lived, but he died too soon. It is as if Ikramullah stopped short of contemplating the future course of this relationship, as if hesitant to sully with raw passion the pristine affection, the intangible bond between the two soulmates. For instance, just before Chooza's death:

> 'Chooze!' Boom said, repeating the time-worn phrase for the millionth time, as if he was the first man on the planet Earth to discover and divulge one of nature's profound secrets.
>
> 'Yes?'
>
> 'Would you mind if I told you something?'
>
> 'Go on.'
>
> 'I don't know why, I'm deeply in love with you, even though I didn't wish it.'
>
> 'I know. I know why. There was this desolate desert, as desolate as deserts can be; there was this scorching sun, as scorching as the sun always is; there was this arduous journey into the interminable unknown, as arduous

journeys into the interminable unknown always are; there was this crashing laughter, as the crash of jeering laughter always is; and two wayfarers in the bleak vastness of the desert—you and me. That's all!'

'That's all?'

'Yes . . . that's all!'

As he uttered those words, Chooza raised his feverish, red-hot hand and touched it to Boom's face. Boom held it and let it stay there, and then he kissed it ever so gently and put it on his breast. The two sat there for the longest time, immobile, silent, lost. The sensation of Boom's throbbing heart travelled through Chooza's hand and continued to be absorbed by his body, penetrating deep into his being.

These, by no means, exhaust Ikramullah's versatility. Short stories such as 'Jangal' and 'Picnic' speak of a writer who is not afraid to experiment with less traditional forms of narration. Though neither narrative has any discernible plot, the intensity of observation and remarkable focus on detail saves them from degenerating into the uninspiring tenor of much of our contemporary symbolic or abstract fiction.

Ikramullah, in Salim-ur-Rahman's apt words, 'does not believe in yielding to pressures applied either by the officialdom or the literary establishment'. And, if for no other reason, he should be read and discussed for 'offending the effete sensibilities of the Pakistani bourgeoisie . . .'

*

Faruq Hassan and I started working on a volume of Ikramullah short stories and novellas sometime in the mid-1990s. My initial idea was to publish it in the Pakistan Writers' Series, Oxford University Press (Karachi), for which I served as general editor. We could only work on our joint project intermittently because of teaching obligations. The translation work progressed very slowly and was completed just a year or two before Faruq Hassan's death in November 2011. Much earlier than that I had already given up my editorship of the series. I submitted the manuscript to R. Sivapriya at Penguin and am thankful to her for her acceptance of the two novellas that appear here. I am also indebted to Ambar Sahil Chatterjee and Arpita Basu for their careful attention to the editing and production of this volume and to Jane A. Shum for going over the manuscript and offering valuable suggestions for improvement.

Finally, I would like to dedicate my part of the work on this volume to the memory of Faruq Hassan—a dear friend and a remarkably kind human being.

1 October 2014 Muhammad Umar Memon
Madison

Regret

Someone called me and gave me Ehsan's message. He said Ehsan wanted me, no matter what, to go see him. He was back from England after his heart surgery. He was annoyed about the fact that I had not gone to see him before he left for England, when he was ailing, and now that he was happy to be back, I must go visit him. He was impatient to meet me.

This happened about ten or twelve years ago. In those days such surgery would not have been available here. Even though he and I have lived in the same city for the past forty or forty-five years and feel affection and fondness for each other, there are times when several years go by without a meeting. And if we do run into each other by chance, we are so wrapped up in our own affairs that after a warm embrace we lapse into talking perfunctorily and, soon afterwards, go our separate ways. In order to live our lives, and in keeping with our domestic and professional—call them social—exigencies, we have unwittingly chosen separate spheres of life for ourselves and have become helplessly trapped in them. Indeed, this has become the way of life in all big cities in the world.

But perhaps this may not be the whole truth, for, in fact, in my case, my wife's obstinacy has also been a major factor. She dreads the man. In fact, she is unwilling to accept him as human. She says human company doesn't make a ghoul human. Many times I have tried to reason with her that Ehsan's physical features have been that way ever since childhood, his strange habits and manner only making his image worse, but that he should not be shunned for his unsightly appearance. Underneath he's a guileless man, indeed a simpleton, without even a trace of artifice in him. By temperament he is sympathetic and high-minded. He talks so sweetly that, on the one hand, he charms his listeners and, on the other, makes them wonder if it is still possible in this day and age for someone to be so candid about himself and others. Then again, he is also a distant relative, a childhood classmate and a friend. I at least enjoy his company and wonder how and why he is so misunderstood. In order to explain the extent of his simplicity and lack of guile, I even told her an incident from our adolescence. In those days a giant-size fried *papar* used to cost a paisa. Ehsan's mamun had given him a rupee on Eid or some other occasion. And what did he do with it? Why, of course, buy papars for the whole rupee and march into my room holding the lot in both hands. He put them in front of me and said, 'Come on, eat.'

Confounded, I looked at his face. 'So many? What are you going to do with all these?'

'Eat them. What else?'

'Even twenty people couldn't finish them off. How will the two of us?'

'Just watch me.'

'Come on. Stop this nonsense. What's the story?'

'No story. For a whole year I have been craving papars but couldn't get hold of even a paisa from anywhere. My mouth watered whenever I passed by the papar-seller's stall. I know if I had asked Aapa for a paisa she wouldn't have refused, but how could I ask her? Farman brings home just thirty-five rupees each month, and Aapa has to stretch them from one month to the next. I know because I'm the one who goes out to buy the groceries. At the end of the month we have to ask the shopkeepers for credit. Three or four months ago I swiped a paisa from the grocery money. When Mother asked me for the account I said one paisa had fallen into a gutter. She didn't say anything. Tucking the paisa under my trouser-belt, I went straight to the papar-seller's. For a long time I stood near him. Finally, I came back with the paisa still intact and put it on Mother's palm. When she asked if I had taken it out of the gutter I said no, it had been with me all along. She said I could keep it if I needed it, but I told her no, I had no use for it. Then I cried, and she cried with me. After that I never thought about papars. Today, when I got a rupee, I thought I should punish my accursed self with a weapon of its choice.'

I ate two papars. He could barely eat ten, all the while cursing his appetite. The rest, all fifty-two of them, we took out and distributed among the beggars and the children in the streets.

My wife laughed derisively and snapped, 'Bravo! That was very smart of your friend, and you should be applauded too for crowing about it. I thought he only looked a fool but he's downright crazy.'

I was saddened to hear her say that. Never before had I thought her capable of such heartlessness. I didn't think a person needed to develop a particular ability to sympathize with others in their suffering or to enjoy, like all good things in life, Ehsan's truthful and candid manner. She had no idea that poverty could show its effect in many ways, all extremely varied.

It's strange. My parents, so long as they were alive, didn't think well of Ehsan either. They weren't afraid of him, but loathed him nonetheless. In our childhood he wasn't allowed to come to our house, and I was also strictly forbidden to see him. In my wife's eyes he was a soul escaped from hell charred inside and out by its intense heat. She said, 'He's ill-omened. He'll spread misfortune wherever he goes and ruin anyone who meets him. For God's sake, stay away from him. Don't ever let him come inside my house or cast his shadow over my children.'

Ehsan had never married, and to preserve my domestic life it was essential for me never to invite him to my home. Because of my wife's constant objections, I finally gave up even visiting him occasionally at his flat. Ehsan never complained about my growing indifference, nor did he insist on continuing the relationship. Although I could sense that he wished I'd continue to see him sometimes, he never said so.

In school he had already failed a few grades. When I passed seventh grade and he flunked eighth, we became classmates. We were friends already, but now became really close. We were also distantly related to each other, but how exactly I could never figure out. Whenever Ehsan's mother, whom he called Aapa, was in a good mood, she would prattle on giving the names of some men and women—who had thought it fitting to leave this world without making our acquaintance—and, linking them to my father and grandfather, would declare us to be related to each other as uncle and nephew, or cousins, or in some other way. Listening to her engrossed in a litany of strange names would surprise us at first, but then we would laugh out loud at the absurdity of those names and the pointlessness of the effort to recall them. In our ignorance we didn't realize that back in those days, middle-class people gave themselves the kinds of names that now the lower classes have started adopting. My father disliked Ehsan's family a great deal. He would turn his face away in disgust whenever Ehsan's father, Bashir Ahmad, was mentioned. Perhaps he thought that now that the family was down on its luck the slightest acknowledgement of their existence might encourage them to borrow money from him. Or perhaps the reason was that in his time Bashir Ahmad had quit his tehsildar's job with the British on the grounds that working for the British was like being a traitor to one's country. He had subsequently joined the Congress party and eventually landed in jail, leaving his family to starve. My father, who felt rather big about his job as reader in an English deputy commissioner's office, might well have resented the slight implied in that act.

We had been classmates for about two months when, during the break one day, I invited him to have qulcha and spicy curried grams with me. He said he never had any money. I told him I had some. We joined the many other students sitting on their haunches in front of the qulcha-and-curried-gram-seller outside the school gates. We bought one qulcha, broke it into two and put the porcelain saucer of curried gram in front of us. A small meatball, as big as an aamla, rolled from side to side in the saucer as each of us formed our morsels, deftly leaving it for the other. Finally I said, 'Ehsan, you have this meatball. I don't want it.'

'No, you take it. I don't eat buffalo meat.'

'Why?'

'I see a live water buffalo in it, all smeared with dung.'

I looked into his eyes to see whether he was telling the truth or just putting me on, and asked, 'Don't you see a live sheep in mutton?' His long, dark, stork-like neck was always stiff. Above it loomed a face with its features chiselled sharply like the edge of a sword. Under his taut skin you could see not only his prominent bones but also the tightness of each tendon. Through his deep purple, thin, pinched and unsmiling lips he said, 'No, I don't.' His small black eyes, frightful and without lashes, constantly darted quick glances in every direction, as though expecting an accident to happen any minute. Besides the fear flashing through them, they carried the unflinching defiance of a dying man resolved to lay down his life for his cause. Perhaps his father, in getting himself hanged for insurgency against the English, had left a noose dangling around his son's neck as well, so that every moment of his life Ehsan waited for the planks to slide from under his feet, and his eyes kept perpetually blazoning that message. I rolled up the meatball in my last bit of bread and put it in my mouth. Its spiciness stung my tongue, like a glow-worm flashing its light two or three times, then it went down my gullet and soon my tongue forgot its pain. When I handed Maula, the qulcha-and-curried-gram-seller, a two-anna piece he gave me back an anna. I suggested to Ehsan, 'Let's buy another qulcha.' But he said, 'No, keep the anna. It'll come in handy some other time.'

With our tongues still burning from the chillies, we walked back into the school yard and stood in the shade of a sheesham tree. In the blazing heat and searing wind, the boys were playing soccer barefooted, kicking up dust in the tiny yard. Whoever got hold of the ball would run with it in whatever direction he liked, while all the other boys tried to stop him. Ehsan took off his cap—which was made of plush, not lambskin as I had mistakenly assumed for a long time—lifted the edge of his militia shirt, and wiped the perspiration off his greenish clean-shaven skull. His head rested on top of a spindly body, scarcely thicker than a bamboo. His cap would constantly slip off his head and land on his ears, its sides buckling under their own weight. He wore it tilted to one side, in the style of his hero Mustapha Kamal Pasha. When he lifted his shirt I noticed that his stomach was as lean as a greyhound's. Above it was an emaciated ribcage. When he breathed, the skin between the ribs moved in and out. Below the ribcage was a small triangular bone which was constantly active. I had a wondrous sensation: Oh, he's very much alive inside!

Ehsan said, 'The English class is about to start. Did you do your homework?'

'Yes, more or less.'

'The British are on their way out. They're losing on every front and the Germans are about to take over. It's the time to study German, yet these stupid instructors insist on teaching us English. I'm not even going to touch English—let Master Zubair kill me if he wants.'

Ehsan's argument was both weighty and quite appealing. There actually was talk everywhere about the imminent defeat of the British, and I thought that if they were sure to go away it was pointless to learn their language. For now, it was wonderful that we would be rid of English; as for German, we'd deal with it when the time came. But Ehsan's argument would've been useless before my father who stuffed English into me with the help of punches and profanities. Ehsan's father was dead. He was free. But mine was alive, and I was his captive.

'Well then, it's settled,' Ehsan said. 'We don't have to go to English class now. The next class is theology; we already know theology. The last period is geography. Well, skipping a couple of classes in a day won't hurt. Let's go for a walk. Tomorrow when we come in we'll submit a note saying we developed a stomach ache during the break today.'

I couldn't say no. Hurriedly we collected our schoolbags from the classroom on the second floor of the decaying, old, fort-like building and quietly sneaked out. The school stood on the edge of the Grand Trunk Road. A narrow side street, which started just opposite the school, went skirting around my neighbourhood, Husainpura, across the railway tracks and crossing, and ended up in the Civil Lines area. Ehsan started off down this road, raising dust with his slippers. I was feeling nervous. What if someone saw me and told my father? I'd have hell to face. Ehsan didn't have to worry about such matters. Everything around us was awash in the yellow, blazing sun. Like Noah's flood the heat was not just pouring down from above, it was spiralling up from below. Our eyes couldn't find comfort anywhere. The dazzling sunlight reflecting off every surface was piercing our eyeballs like needles. The wind was searing. Even the tarred surface of the road had begun to melt. The houses of the residents of my neighbourhood were lined up on our right. On our left we first passed Sufi Nazir's factory and then the bungalows of Shaikh Aftab, Professor Jafri and Mr Pick. These were followed by the high forbidding walls of the leather-goods warehouses and the power-loom factories which were emitting heat along with the muted whirring of their machines. A water pump the size of a mailbox, which had been installed by the committee, was noisily hurling water against a grave-like cement platform. Ehsan put his cap on the faucet, splashed water on his hands and face, and then rubbed his wet hands on his shaven head. Meanwhile, I felt as though I was suspended on a cross out of fear of being caught, scarcely able to even think of cooling myself down with water. Hiding my face behind my schoolbag, I kept walking, hugging the wall. As I passed by my alley I scarcely stole a glance at it. In the empty alley double-storeyed houses of red brick stood shoulder to shoulder, quietly baking in the merciless sun. The green, blue and white upper-storey windows stood silently behind screens fashioned from thin bamboo reeds. They must have been shut firmly to keep out the searing heat. The thought that the windows in my house would also be shut gave me a little courage. Melon peels had blocked the narrow cement gutter running along the unpaved alleyway and dirty water was running everywhere. At the intersection the qulfi-seller, a piece of cloth over his head, was sitting on a long wooden board attached to a wall and dozing off in its shade. The large earthen pot of qulfis on his cart was covered with a wet piece of red rag. He'd straighten up now and then, call out his product, and then sink back into himself again. Taking strides as long as a camel's, Ehsan caught up with me.

'It's a scorcher today, yaar.'

'That's for sure.'

'Let's go to Cold Well and drink some water.'

'That's too far. I have to be home by the time school lets out.'

'It's not that far, Saeed. You're worrying for nothing. If we cut through Company Bagh, it's just on the other side.'

The gate was closing just as we reached the railroad crossing but the pedestrian passage was, of course, still open and some men carrying their bicycles aloft were passing through the turnstile. Ehsan said, 'Yaar, the train's coming. Let's watch it. Then we'll go.'

'Your house is right by the tracks. Haven't you watched enough trains already?'

'No, that's not it. What kind of train at this time—that's what I want to know.'

'If it isn't a passenger train, it'll be a freight train. What of it? Let's go.'

'It won't take more than two minutes. Let's watch it. It'll be fun. Every passing train makes me want to hop on and ride off somewhere far away.'

'You've travelled so much already—Mianwali, Multan, Montgomery, Lahore, you've been to all of them. Still not satisfied?'

'The only journey I remember is the last one, when I went to Lahore Central Jail. I was ten at the time. I don't remember any of the others. I was far too young.'

The gatekeeper inserted two keys into the iron box near the tracks. The bell that had been ringing continuously stopped. When he turned around Ehsan greeted him with a loud 'Assalam-o-alaikum, maulvi sahib.' The maulvi gave him a close look, straining to recognize him. Perhaps he was an old student. Then holding the paan-spittle in his mouth, he raised his face skyward and responded, 'Wa alaikumas salaam.' Ever since I could remember, I had been watching the maulvi in his blue uniform lowering and raising the crossing barriers. On the other side of the network of tracks, along the railway's boundary wall, stood the eight-by-ten-foot platform the maulvi used as a mosque, a fringe of whitewashed bricks running around it to mark the area. There he led the faithful to prayer five times a day and taught the Holy Qur'an to the children in the morning. Everybody called him the 'Hindustani maulvi'. As soon as the engine poked its head out a little way from the signalman's post, the maulvi, wearing his thick, squeaking, *poorbi* shoes, fashioned from local leather and soaked in oil, hustled into his one-room living quarter, a small empty space, the front of which had been turned into a courtyard by hanging a jute curtain around it on a barbed wire. He lifted the curtain, entered the courtyard, and grabbed the signal flags from the cot. Then he came out and walked over to stand in readiness, green flag in hand, a little beyond the gate, in front of the brick watchman's post that looked like a box facing the tracks. Now even the pedestrians and bike riders had stopped crossing, and the whitewashed bricks across the tracks had become more glaringly visible in the pale sunlight. On this side shimmered the maulvi's long, black, oil-soaked beard and his heavy poorbi shoes. The blue uniform came from the British, while the shoes were Eastern. The oil and the mosque were local. The long beard with no moustache was the maulvi's own.

The chugging engine was steaming ahead in all its glory. It gave a warning whistle. A puff of steam flew upward. The sharp whistle went through the still sea of sunlight like a spear and then the sun was as blinding as ever. As he shovelled the coal, the fireman in front of the open pit of the boiler looked like a burning white flame himself. A leather water bag tied to the boiler's door handle swung along with the engine's movement. The engineer was stationed in the midst of the heat unperturbed.

Ehsan said, 'It's the army special. No wonder I couldn't figure out what train was passing through at this time!' As the railcars whizzed by I saw men clad in army uniforms moving about inside. The train picked up speed. The noise of the rolling wheels became louder. Dust rose. Ehsan shouted, 'Fellows, don't become fodder for the guns! Why lose your lives for a mere twenty rupees? Go back.' The train passed. I shuddered at Ehsan's exhortations. He was going to be caught, and so was I. My father would skin me alive. This was the very reason he had forbidden me to fraternize with Ehsan. The fellow was dangerous, no doubt about that. The bell began ringing again. The maulvi removed the keys from the box where he had inserted them earlier and went to raise the barriers. We started crossing the tracks, which were embedded in the road like the circuits of a transistor radio. Two or three tongas and a lorry chock-full of peasants stood on the road waiting for the gates to open. Having shoved coals into the gas cylinder at the back of the lorry, the driver's assistant, wiping off perspiration, was now busily blowing air into the cylinder through a bellows. It took the lorry another couple of minutes after the gates were opened to be fully ready to move.

On our right, for about seventy or eighty yards, a low barracks made of small bricks ran parallel to Hukam Singh Road. Behind it were two other similar barracks, and beyond them a fairly wide parade ground. Guava, mango and plum orchards were spread out for quite some distance along the edge of the ground and the train tracks. Opposite the orchards and across the tracks were the Muslim neighbourhoods of Husainpura, Sharifpura and Tehsilpura, in that order, and at the end of the barracks there was a huge sprawling banyan tree, with the building of the Special Police, the prison and the living quarters of the officer-in-charge around it. The shade of the banyan was for everybody. Some people could always be found under it playing 'cops and robbers', taking the game for real. A little way from the road, on the left, were the rear walls of some bungalows. A round, arched and closed cement embankment—which suddenly emerged from the bowels of the earth at some point and disappeared just as mysteriously near the railway crossing—ran alongside the road. As children we had heard that it carried water to the reservoirs of the Darbar Sahib, but we never could confirm it for ourselves. Once we reached the age when we could have verified it, the partition of the country changed the set-up of everything around us.

We reached the banyan and continued on towards the handpump. After we had our fill of water, the tree's shade felt so cool and comforting that we plunked down to rest for a while on some of the bricks that lay around. Suddenly screams, cries and the sound of desperate pleading—as though someone were being slaughtered—rose from behind the prison walls, along with the sounds of slapping and heavy swearing. I stood up and looked at Ehsan. He said, 'Sit down. It's no big deal. The police are interrogating somebody.'

I said, 'No, let's leave now.'

Just then a policeman emerged from the prison and we saw him dart off towards the office. When he noticed us he yelled, 'Aye, what are you doing here? Get lost.' We were back on the road again.

I asked, 'Ehsan, was this how the police interrogated your father when they arrested him?'

'Man, you're a real dolt. My father wasn't a common thief or a dacoit; he was a fighter for India's freedom. He openly declared his crime the very first day he raised the cry "Long Live Revolution". What could the police interrogate him about when he had nothing to hide? Of course they found ways of harassing him in jail, but that was a different kind of punishment. For example, they would deny him food, put him in solitary confinement, withhold medication when he fell ill, prohibit visits, hold back his mail, deny him B class, subject him to hard labour and so on.'

'But those punishments couldn't be as severe as these beatings.'

'Kiddo, you know nothing; you'd have screamed your head off in a day. You think going through solitary is child's play? That's the toughest of all punishments. Even the hardest nuts get cracked under it.'

I was far from being convinced. Since the matter concerned his deceased father, I merely expressed surprise and kept quiet. Taking slow measured steps, like slumbering horses ambling along a familiar track, braving the searing wind and enduring the prickly needles of sunlight, we reached Company Bagh.

The incredibly pungent odour of the flowers and trees—so pungent, it smelled like hot spices—greeted us, penetrating our nostrils. We didn't mind it, but we didn't feel exhilarated by it either since the blinding light of the sun had by now sucked every drop of freshness from it. A pack of cigarettes lay glistening in the sun on the other side of the street.

Ehsan dashed to it, picked it up and opened it. It was

empty, as expected. He shoved it into his pocket. Neither he nor I smoked, but collecting empty cigarette packs was an obsession of his. We all have our own. It was a very personal craze, though sometimes out of affection he would let me share in it. Three or four shoeboxes, which he had stashed like a treasure in the space between the ceiling of his room and its crooked brown rafters, were chock-full of just such packs. He was absolutely sure no one knew about their existence. One day as he stepped into the house he saw his older sister, Safia, with one of the boxes, which she had removed from its place. She was sitting on the cot and poking through it. At one time Safia was a teacher in an elementary school. Then someone snitched about her father being a Congressite who had died in jail, and she was fired from her job. At first Ehsan was stunned by her prying, and then he started to cry. She laughed, just as the person who had snitched on her at the school must have laughed, while he was crying, just as she or rather the whole household had cried when she was fired. She said, 'Come on, take your box. I was just looking at it. I swear I didn't take anything. I promise I won't touch any of your things again. Forgive me.'

Going around the Purdah Club, we came on to the road that lay in the dusky shade of some thick trees. I said, 'Nice and cool! Aah!'

'See? That's why I wanted you to come. On our day off I sometimes come and sit here the whole afternoon.'

'All alone?'

'Why not?'

'Doing what?'

'Nothing much. Just sitting around.'

I could see on his face that he regretted letting me share

that secret of his; perhaps he was afraid I would talk to others about his abnormal quirky behaviour. So, to cover himself, he added, 'The reading room of the Ranjit Singh Library opens at four-thirty; I go there to browse through newspapers.'

'Ranjit Singh Library?'

'Yeah.'

The buildings around here, all of them, had been put up by Ranjit Singh for his Ram Bagh. Some of them now housed clubs for the native and British officers. The finest of them all, which Ranjit Singh had probably built for his own living quarters, now housed the library. In another building right across from the library, also erected by him, was the women's Purdah Club, and in yet another of his buildings, the offices of the Municipal Committee for the management of the Bagh were located. One building near the Bagh had been added to the Civil Hospital. Ram Bagh was spread over a huge area at one time. It began where its gate now stood. It was apparent from the name of the gate that it had served as the entrance to the Bagh from the city side, which could not have been more than three-quarters of a mile away from where we stood. The British had reduced the size of the area of the Bagh and renamed it Company Bagh.

'Why on earth is it called Company Bagh? Was any particular company given the contract to build it, one that raked in money by selling entrance tickets to it?'

'Don't know why the Angrez called it that. They could have just as easily named it Committee Bagh, after the committee that oversees its management. That would have made more sense. Maybe it's called Company Bagh because people come here in groups, in the company of other people.'

'That makes no sense. A person can also come here alone, the way you do . . .'

We couldn't figure that one out and moved on, still wrestling with the puzzle. In the meantime a carriage transporting children home from school passed us by, and two more soon after.

'School's over,' I said. 'Let's go back.'

'The younger children get off sooner. Our school lets out at the time the call for the Zuhr prayer goes up. There's still time. You can walk a little faster, though.'

Five or six boys, our age, carrying schoolbags and clad in neat khaki shorts and white shirts, whizzed by us on their bicycles talking in English. Ehsan asked me, 'Do you know which school they go to?'

'No.'

'They go to the school run by the Christian missionaries, the one at the end of the Mall. You know what? There they start teaching English from grade one. And they teach all the subjects in English.'

'But, yaar, how could they teach Urdu in English?'

'You dummy! Why would they need to teach Urdu? All you need to know is English, to become a government official. But just watch what happens to these fellows when the Germans take over. Poor fellows, they'll become very much like us—neither of us knowing any German. They'll curse all that time they wasted studying English. Instead, they should've seen a bit of the world. Hey, Saeed, guess what the fees are like at that school!'

I took a long shot and said, 'About ten rupees a month?'

'*Ten* rupees a month? Are you crazy? It's fifty rupees. Got it?'

'Come on, yaar, it can't be. That's about as much as my father makes in a whole month.'

'And that's why you go to that lousy school—no better than an orphanage. And their school—it's like a plush bungalow in the middle of a huge park.'

'Who told you all this?'

'Well, I saw the school by chance; I just wandered by it one day as I was walking on the Mall. Have you heard the name of Lala Krishan Lal, Advocate, the one who is the president of the City Congress?'

'No.'

'Well, it doesn't matter. In the old days, Farman and I used to go to his home to ask him to find a job for Safia. Then later, when she was fired from her job, we used to go there to try to get her reinstated. That's how I became friends with his son, Kishore. He also goes to that same school. He told me all these things.'

'Do you still go to Lala's?'

'Only when we have some problem. He's a very kind man.'

The two of us came out of the Bagh's eastern gate, crossed the narrow Mall Road made desolate by the heat and the sun, and walked over to the small Cold Well. It lay under the foliage of some thick green trees, shaded by a tin shed. Its mouth, about seven feet in diameter, had been divided in the middle by a board: one side reserved for Hindus and Sikhs to drink from, the other for Muslims. Its outer wall was about four feet high, with a small platform around it. A man used to sit all day long on the Hindu side of the well, offering water in crystal glasses. On the opposite side, a tin cup, secured by a chain to a steel drum, rested on the platform for the use of the Muslims. In the evenings, when visitors came in large numbers, a Muslim attendant also showed up. A channel flowed into this yard—about a *kanal* or kanal and a half in size—from its eastern side, carrying water from a canal. A smallish mosque stood by the bank of the channel, and a shop, whose owner was a Hindu, was located in the western corner. He sold puris in the evening, and both Hindus and Muslims ate them without any qualms. When we passed by the shop, chickpeas were boiling in a cauldron and potatoes in a wok. Two workers were busy kneading flour while the owner, having planted himself on a metal chair, was reading the Lahore-based Hindu newspaper *Veer Bharat*. We drank to our heart's content from the tin cup. The water was so cold and so sweet that it refreshed us completely. We never ceased to wonder how on earth wells could produce such cold water in this heat—water even colder than ice water. We experienced the same surprise that day too. Ehsan asked, 'So what do you think—was it worth coming here?'

'Yes.'

'I'll go fetch the newspaper from Lala,' he said. So he did. We sat down on the edge of the channel and began browsing through it. The paper had the usual fare: news of skirmishes between the Japanese and the Allied forces on the Burmese border, in the Assamese hills, in the tribal regions of Imphal and in other areas. Ehsan had another favourite hero besides Mustapha Kamal Pasha. He was General Rommel, the man who had scored victory after victory against the Allied forces. Ehsan was absolutely convinced that Rommel was invincible. His devotion to the General had reached such a point that Ehsan had even begun to see halos around the General's head in pictures. But Rommel had returned to Berlin after suffering a defeat in Africa and dispatching his forces to

Italy, and it was all quiet on that front, so there was no news about him in the paper. Ehsan took it from my hands and went over it again from end to end, only to be disappointed at not finding the news he desired. 'I don't believe that he was defeated there,' he said. 'His retreat may have been a tactical move. And if he's really been defeated, then surely Hitler has stabbed him in the back, jealous as he must have been at all his victories. Rommel has to return to Africa to conquer Egypt and occupy the Suez. Unless he does that, the Japanese army and the Indian National Army won't be able to invade India through Burma, and the British won't be ousted from India.'

The news of the Bengal famine, including three pictures, appeared on one of the inside pages. One of the pictures showed the half-naked skeleton of a woman lying dead under a huge banyan with a small sack lying close to her head. An equally emaciated child sat near her and was trying to wake her up as two men riding their bicycles passed by the corpse and the child. The second picture showed an old man, fallen by the roadside, face down, still holding a staff in his hand, either dying or already dead, and a caravan of starved, half-naked people moving along, leaving him behind. The third was of a famished eleven-year-old girl, her agony and helplessness etched on her face. She seemed unable to do anything about her drooping shoulders, her dangling arms and tilting neck. Only her large desolate eyes showed any signs at all of life.

'There is still hope in her eyes,' I said. 'Timely help may yet save her.'

'I saw my father in jail four days before he died,' Ehsan said. 'TB had made his body as thin as this girl's, and he had hope in his eyes too, just like in hers. But he was dying. And he did die four days later. Eyes are perhaps the last things that die.'

I began reading the news of the famine. The price of rice had shot up from seven and a half rupees to fifty rupees a maund. The irresponsible transfer of stockpiles of rice to the battlefront and to foreign countries was identified as the cause of the famine, and the Muslim League government of Bengal was held responsible for its failure to alleviate the sufferings of the victims. In Ehsan's eyes, the Muslim Leaguers were the lackeys of the British, for whom the death of 400 million Indians meant absolutely nothing.

'We're merely insects in the eyes of the English, not human beings. I feel like taking off for Bengal,' Ehsan said.

'Do you have anything to feed the starving?'

'No, nothing at all. But at least I'll die, like they're dying.'

Just then I spotted the maulvi, who was standing by the channel drying himself with a clod of earth after urinating. I said to Ehsan, 'Get up, let's go. The maulvi is getting ready to give the call for the Zuhr prayer.'

Ehsan returned the newspaper to Lala. We noticed that inside the shop the workers had finished kneading the flour for the puris.

Tucking our schoolbags under our arms, we started back, walking briskly along the Mall that ran parallel to Company Bagh. I don't know what Ehsan was pondering about, but I had only one thought hovering inside my mind—why did Ehsan need to go to Bengal? As it was, he was starving here and might well starve to death one day. Passing by the girls' college we saw the students piling into tongas and buggies to go home. Some unfortunate ones, like us, were trudging along on foot in the scorching sun. Entering through the second eastern gate of the Bagh, which was straight across from the college, we found ourselves back inside. We passed by a bunch of girls without once turning around to look at them. Firstly, because the sun was too hot and, secondly, because nature hadn't yet fitted our eyes with those lenses that suddenly make girls look colourful and smart. It wasn't that they were altogether beneath our notice; to us they seemed rather like the small paper flags fluttering in the wind in front of the cinema halls. In a strong wind some of those flags would tear and even fly away, without causing any grief to anybody. By the way, in those days some strange thoughts did flicker and crawl out of the ant holes of my mind, like, why not stand on my head and call those girls? Near the edge of the road I spotted an empty cigarette packet. I ran and picked it up and showed it to Ehsan. He looked at it casually and said, 'Useless. I already have two or three like this one. Throw it away.' At the rejection of my gift I looked at him with eyes like a hungry pup staring at someone eating in the hope of getting a morsel. At least I felt that way. Ehsan said, 'Newer and unusual packets from truly marvellous brands, with pictures, are found only near the railroad tracks. We'll look for them there.'

When we got back to the railroad crossing, Ehsan turned towards his house, walking on the dirt path alongside the tangle of cables which lay bending away from the railway lines. He was avoiding the signal cables that ran just above the ground towards the outer signal. His was the first house in a row of six or seven nondescript ones facing the tracks about a hundred and fifty yards beyond that outer signal. Orchards sprawled out on three sides of this cluster of houses, while the train tracks stood right in front, and beyond them was Sharifpura and the rest of the city. The houses of Sharifpura were quite near the tracks, their backs facing the tracks like a high, impenetrable, forbidding wall. At the tracks I paused between the gates of the crossing to look at Ehsan as he made his way home. The six tracks, resting upon thick gravel of grey stone, were diligently engaged in the pointless task of refracting the sunlight, throwing it, fountain-like, back into the ocean of light. In this blinding glare Ehsan continued on, walking along the wild growth of *bhang-bathu* in the dusty, lifeless shade of the plum trees. With every step the flapping sound of his slippers could be heard, and dust, as hot as sand in an oven, flew up and fell on to his feet. In the distance, the white outer signal stood against the hazy faded-blue sky like an extended arm barring the way. In this barren landscape, all I could see was this one person advancing towards the southwestward-leaning sun, taking its onslaught directly on his face, his head bent like a porter's.

The monthly rent for Ehsan's house was five rupees. Inside, there was a triangular concrete veranda with two pillars, but the floors of the two rooms, the courtyard and the vestibule behind it were unpaved. A crude bathroom had been fashioned out of the empty space under the stairwell by hanging a curtain over it. The Municipal Committee had largely ignored this settlement. The gutters flowing out of the houses emptied into whatever low-lying spots they could find. Electricity hadn't reached here yet, though it had been available in the city for the past thirty years. Ehsan's mother would laugh and ask me, 'Aye, Saeed, ask your father to get us a permit for kerosene oil. Ask him to have it made for a whole canister. It shouldn't be hard for him; after all, he works in the deputy commissioner's office. On second thoughts, don't bother. I'll come to your house and ask him myself.' But she never did visit us with that request. Her courageous ability to laugh at things through her toothless mouth, in spite of the incredible suffering she had endured all alone, never ceased to amaze me. And when she really burst into laughter, she always made sure to cover her mouth with her dupatta. She had a large face and a wide forehead. The colour of her skin was as pristine white as motia flowers in full bloom. Her body was heavyset. She was very sensitive to the heat. Her perspiration-soaked white muslin shirt would cling to her back, and she would continually cool herself with a small handheld fan. Ehsan's father had owned a huge three-storeyed haveli inside the city. It had been built by his grandfather in prosperous times in the past. After Ehsan's father was fired from his job, they had to sell it in order to meet the family's household expenses, pursue the various court cases, and be able to visit him in jails in distant cities. They were forced to move from those spacious quarters, easily worth a hundred rupees a month in rent, to this house with a monthly rent of five rupees.

Like any other afternoon, a heavy stale odour hit my nostrils as soon as I entered our lane. I slowly climbed the stairs of my house near the chowk and went into my room, the windows of which opened on to the next lane. I dropped off my schoolbag and climbed another flight of stairs to the room where my mother was sleeping, oblivious to everything, with my sisters on either side of her. Her handheld fan had fallen on one side. A wrought-iron grating covered a square opening on the floor to let the breeze flow through to the floor below. Children's legs and other small objects could easily slip through it. The small objects would, of course, go straight down and land in the courtyard on the lower level; the children, on the other hand, would get caught in the grating, fall down and cry for a while, but then learn to walk along the side. Jumping across the grating, I went over to the hearth in the corner. First I downed a whole glass of water from the new clay pitcher. In a wicker basket lay two rotis, and there was some curry with two potatoes and a small piece of meat in an engraved copper bowl—my share of the meal. I had a headache and could only swallow a few mouthfuls. In front, on the clothes line, two of my father's shirts and pants, as dry as a crisp papar, were flapping around in the wind. At four, my mother, half awake and half asleep, would heat up the coal-iron and press these.

Our school closed for summer vacation a few months later. Except for Sundays, Ehsan and I spent every day together until four o'clock in the afternoon. He would come to my house in the morning and the two of us would just sit around in my room—it had a very low ceiling and looked like a box—either gossiping, or occasionally, doing some of the homework assigned for the holidays. Sometimes I would start reading one of the storybooks which I had gotten from a pushcart vendor in exchange for my old seventh-grade books. Ehsan had absolutely no interest in stories. Tales of genies and fairies, hardships endured by princes, the agonies of princesses separated from their lovers—all of these were meaningless to him. He went after solid facts, like the things found in the books on history and politics which he wanted to read but which were beyond our means, and which I had no interest in whatsoever. Sometimes we would go out on a stroll to the outlying areas of the town. I had to get back home before my father returned, and equally important, Ehsan had to be out of my house by then. I can't speak for Ehsan, but I wasn't under any pressure to study or do household chores. Although I enjoyed having a fair amount of freedom, lately I'd begun to feel a strange uneasiness, a nameless anxiety. I wanted something to happen. But what? That was always shrouded in mist and never became clear. The things my parents talked about began to sound false and hollow. I began to hate my house and often wondered if I should leave it and run away. One day I happened upon my sisters' doll chest. I shredded their dolls into bits with scissors. My sisters cried, my mother got angry, but I kept smiling, unperturbed, and went down the stairs into the lane.

The windows of my room opened on to the street some eight or nine feet below. A huge house, which looked even taller from my low-ceilinged room, stood facing my windows across the eighteen feet of the lane. Its four tall windows, door-length high and always covered by yellow reed screens, opened a little higher on to the same lane. There was no boy our age in that house, just a thin, tawny matchstick of a girl, Parveen, who had made it to the eighth grade like us. The only other people to be seen in that house in the daytime were a few women of assorted ages, though in the evening one did see two or three men entering the house, tired from their day's work. At first Parveen didn't even seem like a proper girl. Looking like a wasted little mouse, she would be seen in the morning capering about in the lane barefoot and humming with a bowl in hand, on her way to buy yogurt. And every evening she would be at Maulvi Daoud the sharbat-seller's place with her *sipara* for her lesson. Because she was a rich man's daughter, her lesson would be over quickly, lasting only a few minutes. While the other twenty-five or thirty boys and girls would sit on folded knees for hours on end on the wooden boards fixed to the maulvi's shop and the adjoining stores, rocking back and forth, loudly memorizing their lessons. For some days now—it didn't escape my notice—Parveen had begun to look more like a woman—her walk had steadied, her dupatta was draped more carefully around her body, and her eyes were cast downward. Watching her come into the lane this way made me feel pity for her—a sprightly and vibrant girl being smothered by womanhood. We would sometimes spy a colourful *aanchal* glimmering behind the yellowing reed screens, or see dark eyes watching our room and us through reeds pushed apart by fingernails. That annoyed me a lot, for Parveen had not been concealed behind a veil yet, nor did any of the other women of her house observe purdah before us. Why, then, this peeking? Was it that she wanted to watch us when we were least likely to be conscious of being watched?

One day Ehsan and I were lying on a mat disconsolate and inert like dead bodies, with books and notebooks scattered around us. We weren't exactly tired or asleep, yet we had scarcely wiggled a finger, much less turned over. We weren't sad or unhappy, just weary. Our souls were frozen senseless by boredom and our minds and bodies were defenceless against it. The lane below was bustling with life, as was the upstairs of my house, and film songs blared from the radio in the house across the way. Whenever possible we savoured those songs, letting each one penetrate through our pores into our very beings. At that moment Kanan Bala was singing in her bold, saucy voice, like a koel hopping from branch to branch. But even this favourite song of ours failed to create the slightest stir in our frozen emotions. We had neither the desire to live, nor the wish to die—we just floated like a pair of dead bodies on the still surface of the lake of weariness. At last, making an extraordinary effort, like a rocket moving out of the gravitational pull of the earth, I shook myself and picked my way slowly up the stairs as if sleepwalking. I grabbed my father's single-barrelled gun and pulled it out of its case. Then, yanking a cartridge out of the ammunition belt, I returned downstairs. I said to Ehsan, who was still sprawled out on the mat, 'Look, this is a gun. There'll be a loud bang when I fire it.'

He sat up in alarm to see what stranger was talking to him. My voice and its tremor were strangers to me as well. I was saying, 'Look, this is a cartridge. This is how you load it into the chamber.' Ehsan screamed, 'No, no, don't fire. You'll hit someone.' I clanked the chamber shut and said, 'This is the safety lock. See, now it's unlatched. Here, I'm cocking the gun.' Ehsan, still sitting, pushed the gun with his hand so that its barrel aimed upward. The gun flew backwards out of my hand, its butt hitting the wall, and then it fell down as if dead on the mat. The room became so filled with the fumes of gunpowder that we began to cough. We were stunned and our ears were ringing. The agitated voices of Hasna the provision-seller and Pheeka the butcher were heard from the lane: 'Bao Saeed, what happened? Say something, man!'

'It was nothing, brother. Just a firecracker.'

Parveen's mother, older sister, sister-in-law, three children and Parveen herself stood framed in the window across the lane like portraits of fear. Her mother was calling to my mother, 'What happened, Saeed's mother?' I came to thc window and said, 'Auntie, it was just a firecracker that went off.'

'Oh Saeed! Whoever sets off such booming firecrackers inside a house? Why not set it off out in the lane if you're itching for it so? Crazy boy, scared the hell out of us for nothing.'

My mother came thumping down the stairs bareheaded and barefooted. She was terribly agitated and nearly out of breath. 'Did anyone get hurt?' she asked.

'No, Auntie, we narrowly escaped,' Ehsan replied.

'Thank God,' she said, holding her head in her hands as she collapsed on to the mat with a thud. At this point we couldn't even use the firecracker as an excuse, for the gun lay on the mat as proof of the crime just like the dead body of a victim, having ripped a portion of the plaster—about six inches in diameter—out of the opposite wall, which had then crumbled into a pile on the floor.

'So, you had your fun, eh? Satisfied now? What if something had happened? What would we have done, eh? See if your father doesn't skin you alive today!'

I was feeling a bit ashamed, also fearful at the thought of the evening's coming reprimand. But, in spite of everything, the thought of having created all that commotion by an intentional act, and the feeling of contentment that followed the disappearance of weariness—made me feel quite good.

It was surprising for me to see signs of fear and astonishment on Ehsan's face. Wasn't he happy to see the end of our boredom? Or perhaps he wasn't bored after all; perhaps I had only assumed that he was as bored as I was. Perhaps he was just lying on the mat dreaming about a past different from what it had actually been. A past in which his father had never joined the Congress party and had never been jailed, in which he and his mother hadn't had to knock about from jail to jail just so that they might visit him. A past in which his father had not died, was still the tehsildar that he had always been, and they still lived in their ancestral mansion, still had their old horse-drawn carriage in which to ride to Cold Well to eat puris every evening, and every morning he himself, like Farman, put on his shoes, had a breakfast of two parathas, drank tea with white, not raw brown, sugar in it, and pedalled away on his bike to the English school to study.

'You rascal, get up and go home,' Mother said to Ehsan. 'And if I ever see you set foot in this house again, you'll be sorry. Sneaking in here like a thief early in the morning, unbeknownst to anyone! You good-for-nothing brat, now you're even ruining our child. Do you ever think of leaving once you're here?'

Ehsan rose from the mat, put on his slippers and shuffled out, dragging his feet. Where before Ehsan used to come to my house, I now started going to his. One day we started out from his house, walking along the train tracks on our way to see Forty Wells. Even though Ehsan warned me that the place was quite far, I didn't listen. The Forty Wells were a great source of fascination for me back then because of the story of Ali Baba and the forty thieves, which I had recently read. I was convinced that the legend's remnants must still be lurking around the Forty Wells. At least a few of the forty thieves must still be there, sitting around in their long flowing robes. Ali Baba himself must have remembered his forty thieves when he heard the name 'Forty Wells' and—who knows?—he might even have gone there. Maybe I'd meet him there. In reality those forty wells were tube wells that the town had installed to meet its water needs. They should have named each well after one of Ali Baba's thieves.

It took a while for us to pass through the Sharifpura neighbourhood, then we entered Tehsilpura. After we had crossed through that, fewer and fewer houses could be seen, until finally, there were none. Dense mango and guava orchards spread out on either side of the train tracks running to infinity on their long raised bed of grey gravel. Ehsan told me that the farther of the two tracks on our right was for trains coming from Delhi and the nearer one was for those going to Delhi. The third set of tracks veered sharply left, towards Pathankot, as it neared Forty Wells. Both the inbound and outbound trains blew a long whistle when they neared that bend. There was a big board by the bend with the word 'WHISTLE' inscribed on it in English, and surely the engineers must have had their orders to blow the whistle at this point. We abandoned the small dirt trail and tried to walk on the tracks. Ehsan's slippers made it difficult for him to keep his balance, so he took them off and tucked them under his arm. Still he tottered once or twice and stepped on the gravel, which made his feet bleed. He put his slippers back on and said, 'Look, if we keep playing around like this we won't be able to get back before the afternoon. Walk fast.' Here the trail had become even narrower because of infrequent use. As we could no longer walk side by side, we started to walk one behind the other. On one side was the gravel and on the other, nearer the higher ground of the orchards, were underbrush and weeds. Sometimes we would hear the watchman's 'Ho, ho' shooing away the birds. These sounds, which sometimes seemed to come from nearby and sometimes from quite far away, had a music all their own—not sad or pained, just conveying a hint of command. We found them pleasing whenever they could be heard, perhaps because they made us aware of the presence of other humans in the forest and lessened our fear of being isolated. Now and then two or three flocks of screeching parrots would fly over our heads from the orchards on one side to those on the other—greenish arrows flying noisily against the blue background of the sky.

'Yaar,' I said, 'can't these parrots fly with their mouths shut? After all, other birds fly too, but none of them creates such a racket. Seems like they're making fun of us.'

'All right, so now it's the parrots you have to pick a quarrel with. If they heard you they'd perch straight across from you on a tree and laugh so hard you'd begin to cry.'

'Parrots talk, but do they also laugh?'

Ehsan broke out laughing. I did too. The issue was lost in our laughter, though it never got resolved.

'Look,' Ehsan said, 'I'm going to cross over to the trail on the other side of the tracks. I haven't spotted even one new cigarette packet since morning. You keep an eye out too.' He went across the tracks to the other side. I noticed two or three birds with feathers as soft and smooth as silk sitting huddled together on the telegraph lines, all puffed up, like rolled cotton balls. I asked, 'What are those birds called, Ehsan?'

'Kaal chiri,' he answered.

He picked up a rock and hurled it. It hit the pole with a 'tunn' and the birds took off. They flew close to the wires, swooping up and sailing down in a wavy motion, then disappeared from sight.

'You made them fly away for no reason,' I said.

'Come here and listen to this. You'll find a lot more birds like that up ahead.' I went and put my ear to the pole.

'Do you hear anything?'

'Yeah, just a jingling—like something's about to happen, but nothing does. It's continuous.'

'That's coming from the cables, it'll keep on like that. I was asking about the "tunn". It sounds different inside the pole. You missed it. Here, try now.'

He picked up a handful of stones from the tracks while I stood ready close by. As soon as he hit the pole with one, I ran and stuck my ear to it. The noise inside the pole didn't sound as sharp as it did outside; it sounded smoother and more rounded, like an echo. Eventually the echo subsided. Ehsan's eagerness and insistence had made me think the experiment would be something like a kaleidoscope for the ears. But it turned out to be nothing of the sort. I listened a second time and a third time, but my opinion remained the same. Disheartened, he began taking aim at the pole with the remaining stones. I joined in the game. We agreed to hurl five stones each from a distance of fifteen steps.

Whoever hit the target more often would be the winner. Suddenly he screamed, 'Look, the train!' I looked. The grandeur of the train approaching full speed was something out of this world. For the first time in my life I stood awestruck, watching this magnificent sight: a jet-black engine hurtling forward, spewing smoke and raising a storm of dust in its wake. In less than a minute, first the engine and then the noisy rattling cars whizzed past us. The fleeting images of faces and quick flashes of fabric colours flitted before our eyes. The earth vibrated for a while and a dust- and straw-laden wind that had picked up made us feel we were in the midst of a squall.

'That was the Bombay Express,' he said. 'Its scheduled arrival at the station is ten-thirty. Looks like it's on time.'

'Did you pick up any packets?' I asked.

'No. The rare ones can't be found here. We've come too far from the station. The kinds I like are found, at the most, no farther than the tracks near my house. We'll have to go to the station some day.'

We crossed back over the tracks to our previous trail, the one we had been trudging along before because it was in the shade, and walked, one behind the other, for about fifteen or twenty minutes. It was a long trek and we had little time left. A water channel, running through the two orchards on the left, passed under the railroad bridge. We stopped to examine the bridge. We were panting and our clothes were soaked in perspiration. The tracks here were laid over iron ties, instead of wooden, and through the open spaces between them we could easily see the muddy fast-moving current below. We kept picking up stones and dropping them into the water, enjoying the 'glup, glup' of the water and its spurts.

'How about catching some fish?'

'There're no fish here,' he said. 'What would you catch? I tried once, using a piece of muslin as a net. The canal-digger wandered by. He said all the fish are caught at the barrage and the big canal. None reaches here.'

I threw a dry leaf in the water and ran to the other side of the bridge. The leaf floated under the bridge and continued on into the channel. I was happy that my leaf was moving forward and was going to travel to the very ends of the earth. Later, another flock of screeching parrots flew overhead. When they were exactly above us, I lifted my face and screeched back. I felt as if the last bird of the flock turned its red beak towards its spindly green tail, looked at me and laughed, and then hurried away. The thought saddened me that should I ever run into this friendly parrot again, I probably wouldn't recognize it at all. I realize today that fellowship is something you cherish in your heart. That parrot is as good a friend of mine today as it was when it turned around to look at me, laughing companionably.

'Let's put an ant on the leaf this time around,' I said. 'As a passenger on our raft.'

'All right. Let's stick two leaves together. The passenger will be happier in a roomier boat.'

Ehsan snipped two mulberry leaves from the orchard. We linked them together with a few dry sticks and shaped them into a funnel. A fat ant was rushing along the trunk of a tree. I grabbed it, put it on our tiny leaf-boat and released the boat into the water. But the boat careened and started to float on its side, allowing water to flow in and out freely. We saw the ant thrash its clumsy-looking legs about in a desperate attempt to save its life in the swift current, but then we couldn't see where the powerful surges of the rushing water took it. I ran over to the other side. The leaf-boat was stuck in the grass on the bank and was empty of its lone traveller. I picked it up, turned it about and looked at it closely. Then I threw it away. We felt sad about the tragic end of the creature we had wanted to be the Vasco da Gama of the ant-world. Inwardly a little peeved with each other, we stood there for a while in hushed silence.

'If only you hadn't tried to be so smart,' I said, 'the ant would have made it to the other side.'

'Why didn't you warn me that the boat would capsize?'

'Didn't you already know that?'

'All right. Let's put an ant on a flat leaf this time.'

Another poor ant was captured and set afloat on the water

on a dry leaf. It reached the other side of the bridge safely and we yelled, 'It's here, it's here.' The way it stood in the middle of the leaf madly rubbing its forelegs together told us that it was neither happy at the free ride nor cared much about adventure. The stupid thing wanted simply to stay alive. For a while we did see it sitting disgruntled on the leaf, sailing away in the middle of the channel, but we don't know what became of it afterwards.

We returned and sat down across from each other on opposite banks and stuck our feet into the cold water. For a while we sat peaceably enough, but then we started splashing water at each other with our feet. To save his cap from getting wet, Ehsan took it off and placed it at a distance. He looked like an entirely different person the minute he stepped out of his Mustapha Kamal Pasha disguise. A fresh wave of exhilaration washed over us with each new splash of water, the heart wishing for more from the enemy. Soon we resorted to splashing water with our hands as well. Our clothes were soaked. I said, 'We have to dry our clothes now.'

'Don't worry,' he said. 'They'll be dry soon. What are summers for?'

'May take longer while you're in them.'

'In that case, let's go across the tracks. We'll take off our clothes and have a swim in the channel. In the meantime the clothes can dry. The current is fast here, and besides, who knows how deep the water is under the bridge! Over there, it only comes up to my belly button, and it probably comes up to your chest at the most.'

We walked across the tracks to the other side of the bridge in our wet clothes, making 'shleping' sounds. Ehsan said, 'You sit down facing Forty Wells and shut your eyes. I'll rinse my clothes, spread them out in the sun and then jump into the channel. Open your eyes when I tell you to. If you cheat even a little, I swear I'll never speak to you again.'

'What's the big deal? I have to spread out my clothes too.'

'I don't know whether you will or not. If you break your promise, I'll start off for home in my wet clothes.'

'All right, all right,' I said. 'Hurry up now.'

It seemed as if a whole century had passed. I asked, 'Should I open my eyes now?'

His voice came from behind me, 'Yeah, go ahead.'

I turned around to look. He stood ten feet away, still fully clothed. 'What happened?' I asked surprised.

He came near me and said, 'Why, those coal-gatherers . . . they're headed straight this way. What could I do?'

Two girls of about fifteen or sixteen, clad in ghagras, were coming along from the direction of the city. Their eyes were focused on the ground between the tracks for the Delhi trains. They were talking slowly as they picked up pieces of half-burnt coals from between the tracks and stuffed them into pouches slung over their necks and dangling behind on their backs. Having walked unshod on the stony gravel for an eternity, their feet had become so calloused they couldn't be injured like Ehsan's. They caught up with us and soon left us behind. I said, 'Go on, their backs are facing us now. You can spread your clothes out to dry. I doubt they would care to look back at you, and you're not a piece of coal they might want to pick up and toss in their pouches.'

Irritated, he said, 'In that case, why don't you go first?'

I took off my shirt and spread it in the sun and then entered the water with my pyjamas on. Covered by the water, I took it off, squeezed it and, still standing in the water, spread it out along the bank.

'Why didn't I think of that?' Ehsan said.

We tried to teach each other how to swim, though neither of us really knew how. Then, like birds, we splashed the water around for some time. The sudden heavy rumble of an approaching engine startled us. Soon the engine and the carriages passed us by like a dream. Ehsan said, 'Frontier Mail—the queen of all trains. It'll be at the station at eleven-thirty.'

I mumbled, 'I only heard it when it was already upon me.' Then I asked Ehsan, 'There were two silver-coloured compartments with some English writing on them, weren't there?'

'Those were the names of the compartments—"Gul-e Yasmin" and "Gul-e Neelofar". Even in this weather it's as cold inside them as it is in December. Only big officers, Englishmen, Rajas and Maharajas travel in them.'

'They must use slabs of ice to keep them that cold.'

'No, they use machines.'

'If they're so cold in summer, they must be freezing in winter.'

Ehsan chuckled. 'The same machines warm them in winter.'

'How do you know? Have you ever travelled in one?'

'No, Mahmood told me. He's my cousin, my maternal uncle's son. He's a captain in the British army. He always travels in that compartment. These days he's stationed at the Imphal border. Aapa says Safia should be married to him. Farman, however, doesn't agree.'

'And you—what do you say?'

'Nobody asks me. But you wouldn't expect me to agree to

my sister marrying someone who's in the army of the English who killed my father, would you?'

'Is he the same uncle who sometimes gives money to your mother?'

'He is the only maternal uncle I have.'

'And is it his wife who comes to your house and starts searching for new purchases to figure out how much money her husband may have given your mother?'

'Yes. Aapa says when the police came to search the house during my father's lifetime, they didn't do as thorough a job as her bhabi does.'

'What a witch, yaar!'

'She finds fault with Aapa all the time. Poor Aapa just sits and listens, never answering back. Once, not long after my father's death, she said to Aapa, "Ever since you married, you've been a burden on us. How long can we go on paying your expenses? First your husband languished in prisons, then, utterly sick of you, he decided to die." Aapa's face contorted in anguish when she heard that and she broke into tears. Seeing her cry, I began to scream and went to the gutter and threw up. Aunt said, "Look at this, not only do they leech off us, they shed tears as well."'

'How then will that woman ever come round to letting her son marry Safia?'

'Mahmood is an only son, and he has told her in so many words that if he ever marries, it will be Safia, or he will not marry at all. Now that her interest is at stake, she's softened a bit lately.'

We stood quietly in the water feeling sorry about this state of affairs and all but forgot our games. At last I broke the silence and said, 'Yaar, I'm dying of hunger.'

'Me too.'

We quickly put on our clothes. In the distance the same girls were now coming back, this time picking up coal from between the Pathankot tracks. Ehsan asked if I had any money on me.

I searched my pocket and screamed with joy, 'Got it! I have an anna.'

'That's plenty. Let's go into the orchard and ask the gardener to sell us some mangoes. After we've eaten them, we'll go home. Let's not go to Forty Wells today. It's getting late.'

Muted light, as at dusk, and cloying silence greeted us inside the orchard after the blinding glare outside. Gigantic sprawling mango trees stood laden with small yellow fruits. The guavas were as green as the leaves, still very small, about the size of tiny balls, and without any hint of fragrance or colour. The plum trees had all been picked; however, now and then a red plum hidden somewhere behind the leaves still showed itself. Patches of furtive dappled golden light fell quietly here and there on the reddish soil, like so many intruders. The smell of trees, fruit and wet earth wafted unseen through the orchard. The cry of 'Ho, ho', very much a part of the orchard's atmosphere, would sometimes rise from a corner and then die down. A clay pellet fired from a fully stretched slingshot was heard whizzing through the leaves and a flock of parrots flew up creating a ruckus, like a pack of mischievous children. The flutter of their wings in flight was a joy to hear and sounded strangely intimate, like one's own heartbeat. Dry leaves crackled and crumbled underfoot. We ignored them and moved on, perhaps because they weren't human. Sometimes a sparrow, a dove or a pair of green pigeons could be seen moving about amid the leaves. Two or three agitated mynah-birds were walking about the grounds as though they had alighted especially to carry out an inspection. I guessed from the birds' movements and their attempt to take shelter in the trees that it must be about one or one-thirty in the afternoon. I said, 'I've never seen a parrot move about, or seek shade at noon.'

'Yes, because they're green.'

'What difference does that make?'

'The Holy Prophet's mausoleum is also green, that's why heat doesn't affect it.'

The reference to such a sanctified and lofty name just about swept me off my feet. We had walked almost to the middle of the orchard now. A middle-aged man wrapped only in a sarong, his belly bulging out, sat on a large cot, smoking a hookah. Baskets full of different varieties of mangoes lay around him. Twenty paces away, a tall, lean, young man, also draped in a sarong and naked from the waist up, sat baking thick rotis on a griddle. The wriggly blue smoke and its acrid smell made us feel a strange regret, tinged with shame. A black-clay pot tied to a string hung from the branch of a mango tree directly above the young man's head. Close to the pot also hung a brand-new water pitcher, its mouth covered with an inverted clay bowl.

Ehsan said, 'Mehr-ji, may we have an anna's worth of mangoes?'

In a royal gesture, as if he were Emperor Akbar, Mehr-ji pointed towards a basket and said, 'Take a bagful.' The mangoes were small and dry. Since Ehsan's shirt hem was larger, he stretched it out and I started filling the makeshift pouch with fistfuls of mangoes. He kept raising the hem up until his navel was bared, and I kept stuffing it with more. Whereupon Mehr shouted, 'Enough, that's enough. It's more than a bag.' Afraid, I pulled back my hands, letting the mangoes drop back into the basket. Ehsan started to walk ahead of me. Coming to a jamun tree, he emptied the pouch at its roots and said, 'Come on. Let's drink some water first.'

'From where?'

'Oh, just come along.' He went back to the gardener. 'Mehr-ji, we'd like to have a drink of water.'

Mehr-ji called out, 'O Rammu, give the boys some water.'

Rammu brought down the pitcher, filled the bowl and gave it to Ehsan. He drank halfway and then handed the bowl to me. We weren't particularly thirsty since we had already swallowed a lot of water during our attempt at swimming. I was still drinking when a cry was heard in the distance, 'Mehr-ji, a thief, a thief!' Straining his back, Rammu rushed off in the direction of the cry saying, 'Mehr-ji, Nikku seems to have caught somebody stealing mangoes.' We sat down, leaning against the tree trunk, and started sucking on our mangoes. Barely five minutes later who do we see filing in but the two coal-gathering girls followed by Rammu and Nikku in his loincloth. Nikku was a boy of about eight or nine. A slingshot as big as he was hung from his shoulder and a cloth bag filled with clay pellets dangled from his neck. The girls' arms and hands were black from coal, even their faces had black smudges on them. A half-eaten mango in hand, they walked along smiling and talking casually, as if nothing special had happened. Their white teeth sparkled between their darkened lips like strings of pearls. Rammu was clearly having fun chiding them. 'So, you thought you could pluck mangoes freely as if the orchard belonged to your father, did you?'

'Oh, go away, we didn't pluck them. They were lying on the ground, rotting. Did the sky fall down because we picked them up?'

Nikku was out of breath, beside himself with emotion. He said, 'Brother Rammu, they're clearly lying. This younger one was standing on the shoulders of the older one plucking from the sindhuri mango tree by the tracks. When I saw them, I yelled and grabbed the older one by the legs. Both of them came tumbling down with a thud. The younger one got up and gave me a few whacks on the back. But I didn't let go.'

'Oh, shut your trap, you little runt. Quit bragging. You aren't more than a couple of inches above the ground. Can you even see anything higher than yourself? We didn't pluck anybody's mangoes.'

Rammu bared his teeth in a cackle and said, 'You'll find out soon enough, when somebody plucks your mangoes.'

In his innocence, Nikku agreed with Rammu chiming in, 'Yeah, then you'll find out.'

The older girl gritted her teeth and fired back, 'Watch your tongue, buster! We're not waifs. The people who look after us aren't dead yet.'

It wasn't just Nikku, at the time even I couldn't understand the reason for the girl's chagrin.

We got up and went to Mehr's cot to watch the spectacle. Nikku started to explain, but Mehr hushed him, 'Wait, Nikku my son. All right, girls, now tell me how many mangoes did you pluck?'

'We didn't pluck any. Just picked up these two from the ground.' They showed the two half-eaten mangoes they were holding in their hands.

'All right, either sit down and make a hundred pellets of

clay, or give me an anna each, or dump all this coal right here.'

Nikku said, 'Mehr-ji, I hope you won't let them go. It'll be fun to watch them roll a hundred pellets each.'

Rammu stood smiling roguishly with his hands on his bare waist. 'It will be night before they're done, if at all. Get up, the clay's over there. Fetch the water from the channel and get started. Way to go!'

They started pleading, 'Mehr-ji, have mercy on us. In God's name, please forgive us. We'll never set foot in your orchard again.'

Suddenly Ehsan said, 'Take four of our mangoes for their two, but please let them go.'

Mehr was annoyed by this interference. 'Two for one, eh? Do you know what the fine is for stealing one mango? It's a hundred mangoes. Do you have two hundred mangoes?'

'No, I don't. But you can take all we have.'

'Mehr-ji, please forgive us. We touch your feet. Now even the fine's been paid.'

'If I see you stealing one more time, you'll get it from me. Go now.'

Before leaving, the older girl looked straight into Ehsan's eyes and said, 'Babu, may God give you a bride as beautiful as the moon,' and then the two fled from the place, like parrots taking flight.

They had, of course, pleaded much, but their faces showed neither repentance nor alarm. Even while they were apologizing, they appeared unaffected by the words they were uttering, as if they were merely going through the motions. Mehr refused to take the mangoes from us and said, 'If we didn't act so strict, the orchard would be ruined before evening.'

During the last few days I had noticed that whenever I visited Ehsan, he would be waiting for me outside on the veranda and we would immediately take off along the tracks, either in the direction of the train station or of Forty Wells. It wasn't like that at all in the past. When I visited him I used to find him puttering around inside the house. Now he even rejected out of hand all my proposals to walk to some street or neighbourhood, or to Company Bagh. It seemed as if he was tied to the railway tracks, his hawk's eyes always searching for something around them—empty cigarette packets, I assumed. Once or twice we ran into the same girls, but they would just titter and walk on. Ehsan became a different person the minute he saw them, a little nervous, a little agitated. If they happened to be far, he tried to catch up with them in a hurry; if they were close by, he tried even more quickly to get away. Back then I didn't know that these were the signs of love. Then again, my mind was somehow fixed on the notion that love was something that happened between princes, fairies, princesses and sons of viziers. It was inconceivable to even imagine that love could sprout between Ehsan and a couple of coal-gatherers. One day, on our way to Forty Wells, we saw them again, walking quite some distance ahead of us. Ehsan nudged me to hurry. We almost ran to catch up with them. By the time they had gotten near the orchard by the channel, the distance between us had shrunk to about a hundred yards. Suddenly Ehsan said, 'Let's go back!' I stared at his face and said in anger, 'What do you mean?' He was a bit taken aback, perhaps less because of the way I'd spoken and more because he had come to the point where he would have to confess one of his weaknesses to me. He kept walking, or rather dragging himself quietly behind me for quite a while. Then he came up next to me and said, 'I'll tell you. The older girl, I want her to be in front of my eyes all the time. I never want to take my eyes off her. But when we do come face-to-face, I get so flustered I want to flee.'

'Come on,' I said laughing. 'Don't give me all that. Let's go talk to them. It feels good to talk to them.'

'At least find out their names.'

'Come on, we'll ask them.'

When we got really close to them, he blurted out, 'Saeed, for God's sake don't ask anything. Let's go back.'

When they heard our voices, they turned around and halted. The Pathankot tracks, curving sharply, were heading off somewhere far away. The vast green field in front was so large it could have swallowed the armies of both Porus and Alexander easily enough. The two tracks for the Delhi trains, scared of the vastness, were moving quietly along one edge. In the empty field off in the distance, an isolated bungalow stood in the scorching sun. The few eucalyptus trees around it couldn't have protected it much. The chain of tube wells started just beyond the bungalow, which housed the office and residence of the superintendent of the wells. The girls were laughing amiably. I went to them and asked, 'You've come so far today?'

The older one said, 'We came looking for coal. And you?'

'Oh, just to see Forty Wells.'

She took a fistful of roasted grams from the end of her chunri, put them in her mouth and started chewing loudly like a she-goat. 'So, go see them,' she said.

'What are your names?' I asked.

'Why do you need to know our names?' the younger of the two asked.

'My friend wants to know.'

'Does your friend not have a tongue in his mouth?' the older one said. 'Why doesn't he come and ask himself?'

I turned around to look at Ehsan. He stood far away near a telegraph pole cowering like a thief.

The younger one also stuffed a fistful of grams into her mouth, and saying, 'The sun is killing me,' she went and sat down in the shade of a big sheesham near the crops at the edge of the fields. The other girl opened the end of her chunri towards me and said, 'Have some. They're nice and hot from the sun.'

I took a fistful and began munching. She then moved towards the sheesham and said, 'You come in the shade too, and ask your friend as well.'

We sat on the ground in a circle. The older one said, smiling, 'You were asking our names. Well, I'm Lali and she's Toti. She's my cousin, my aunt's daughter, and a friend as well. Anything else?'

Ehsan raised his eyes, once, to look at Lali's face, and then lowered them. Surprised, I asked, 'That's all? Lali, Toti—nothing before or after?'

'What more could there be?'

I became quiet. I was under the impression that 'Begam' or 'Khanam' was appended to every woman's name. But then it occurred to me that such tags would really have ill suited names like Lali and Toti.

'You've been coming around here for some days now. Where did you scavenge for coal before?'

'In the railway yard. That place has plenty. We could fill three or four bags in a day. Here we have to walk for miles and yet find very little, scarcely enough to fill one bag. In the yard, although the place is very small, many engines come and go several times a day. Every two or three hours when they stir the furnace with the fork, a lot of coals tumble out along with the ashes.'

'So why did you quit going there?'

'Come, Toti, you tell them. I can't.'

'There was a lineman there, as black as an engine. He wanted Lali to sleep with him or never come there again to pick up coal. We went up the stairs to the balcony to see the head-lineman. When he heard us out he laughed, "Well then, go and sleep with him." When Lali started crying, he said, "All right, don't. What do you want me to say?" When we complained to an engine-master about it, he also laughed and said, "Nothing strange about that, is there? What have you got to lose? On the other hand, it would please him very much." Then we went to the Big Sahib, you know the one who gets pushed up and down the tracks on a trolley. The men who pushed his trolley turned their faces and snickered. The sahib snapped, "No one is allowed to pick coal in the yard. The man was right to stop you. You people use it as an excuse to steal railroad property. Watch it, or I'll have you locked up." Nobody listened to us. It was so easy to pick up coal there; we weren't about to call it quits so easily. So we didn't show up for a few days. But then greed got the better of us. We thought the lineman must have forgotten all about Lali by then. So we returned. We had gathered only a little bit of coal when the same lineman showed up. He said, "I knew you wouldn't be able to stay away, that you'd be back. You even complained to the big boss. Did anything happen? Come this way now." He had come out of the room below the balcony which always remained closed. That day the door was open. Lali turned pale. She grabbed a couple of rocks from the tracks. When he came to take her by the arm she hurled a rock at him. It hit his forehead, which started bleeding. He slumped over right there. We dropped our bags and took to our heels, stopping only when we'd gotten to our tents. We haven't returned to that place since.'

Just as soon as the story started, Ehsan, who had been sitting there ill at ease until then, was drawn into it, and before long, he was completely engrossed. If a deaf person were there he would have understood the whole story just by watching the expressions on Ehsan's face. His nostrils flared up and he asked, 'What is the name of that lineman?'

Lali said, 'Why? Are you going to go fight with him? What will you do with his name? Forget it.'

I asked, 'Didn't the men in your family do anything about it?'

'Nobody asked us and we didn't say anything,' Lali said. 'What good would it have done anyway? We are *changars*. Our men lie about in the tents, drugged, day and night. They don't do any work. They couldn't care less how their women make a living. Only if a woman ran away would they risk everything to bring her back. Of course, they can't let go of their means of livelihood. Our marriages are all arranged within the tribe. Like Toti, here, she's getting married to my brother.'

Feeling bashful, Toti hid her face in Lali's shoulder. She said, 'Oh shush, Lali, or I'll tell them that you're marrying my brother.'

'We people raise chickens, goats and donkeys, and sell them. Our women look after all the work. The only thing our men get involved in is petty larceny—that is, if an opportunity offers itself. The women make toy elephants and horses with waste paper, straw and scraps of cloth. They weave winnowing fans and mould clay toys that are baked in kilns. The older women go from street to street selling these things. We also make clay ovens. We can do every kind of work. If there is no work, we even beg for alms. We work day and night, but even then we get only one meal a day. Wherever there's a festival or a fair, we load our wares on the animals and go. Like two and a half months ago we came here for the Baisakhi fair, and we'll move on to some other place in a few days.'

Oblivious to everything else, Ehsan was listening to Lali talk. I said, 'The Frontier Mail went by long ago. It must be one o'clock. Get up, let's get going.'

'Lali, I'm dying of thirst,' Toti said. 'Let's find some water first.'

But Lali was asking Ehsan, 'Why were you offering that fat man all your mangoes that day?'

'Why, he was humiliating you, wasn't he?'

For a brief moment a smile, filled at once with gratitude and a curious awareness of her own smallness, appeared on her face, but then she became dead serious. Staring Ehsan straight in the face she stood up to her full height before him, as if with her next move she would step into him and lose herself completely. 'How many of them would you stop from humiliating me?' she said. 'Humiliation has been my companion since birth. It's been my twin.'

Ehsan said, 'Don't let it upset you. God doesn't create people less worthy or more worthy of honour. It's the powerful and selfish who make them so, in order to exploit the weak. The revolution will set everything right.' He was speaking Farman's language.

'Nothing will happen. Such is our lot in life. Nobody can do anything about it.' Then she looked at Ehsan and said, 'Come again tomorrow. The same place. Now go. We'll go separately. If you accompany us, people will make fun of you.' She started laughing again.

The next day when I got to Ehsan's house at my usual time, Safia said, 'He was here on the veranda a little while ago, walking up and down, up and down.'

'He isn't here any more.'

'Then he must have stepped out.'

'Where to?'

'When you go out with him on your rounds every day, do you tell me where you're going?'

Feeling a little ashamed, I started to go. She jeered, 'Tut, tut. All alone, what will you do today?'

'Something. You be quiet.'

She began to chuckle. Ehsan's mother said, 'Safia, you brought the boy almost to tears. Don't do that, daughter. He comes here so devotedly.' Then she said to me, 'Come, Saeed. Sit down here, son. Ehsan will be along soon.'

But I didn't sit there. I returned home, feeling resentful at his fickleness. Now I realize that my resentment was out of place. On my way home, despite my annoyance, I kept thinking of the time when he had started crying in the midst of singing. That morning we had gone out on our stroll. Eventually we ended up at the Darbar Sahib. First we completed a circuit of the pool and then we crossed over the bridge and stepped into the Harmandar Sahib, built right in the middle of the pool. The high, bright marble edifice with its golden dome stood glistening in the sun. The marbled walls and hallways had colourful floral inlays, just like in Muslim architecture. But there were also some peacocks, pigeons and parrots, fashioned out of the same material. On the altar, the highest place, a *granthi* sat reading from the Granth Sahib while a man standing behind him, fanned it respectfully with a *churi*. Below sat a band of singers, chanting hymns. Devotees came, touched the ground in front of the holy book with their foreheads and sat down for a while, listening reverentially to the hymn-singing. Then they went and lined up in front of the man who was handing out *karah-parshaad*. Reverently they extended both their hands, received the parshaad and moved on. I was looking for some idol there. When I didn't see any, I thought they must keep it hidden and only bring it out at appropriate times. In those days idol-worship was believed to be part of every religion except Islam. No one was talking inside the Harmandar Sahib. Tongue-tied from awe and dread we stood respectfully for some time, all the while afraid—at least I was—lest someone should step forward and say, hey, these are Muslas, get them. And then only God knows what kind of treatment we would have been subjected to. On the way out we didn't touch the ground with our foreheads, but like the others, did receive our tiny share of the karah-parshaad. I was watching Ehsan, waiting for him to eat his so that I might eat mine. At last we came out of the Darbar Sahib with our fists still closed. When I was about to eat my share, Ehsan said, 'Wait, yaar, let me think. We're Muslims. Should we be eating this at all?'

'It doesn't have any meat in it, so we needn't worry about whether the animal was properly slaughtered.'

'You probably don't know this, but after frying halva the Sikhs slash at it vigorously with swords to make it what we'd call *jhatka*.'

'But halva isn't anything living that could be slaughtered, is it? It would still be halva.' Saying this I slipped it into my mouth. Ehsan stood thinking for a while, but then he too ate his. Swallowing it, I said, 'Wasn't much, was it?'

'*Tabarruk* is always like that. It's not to fill your stomach.'

'Yaar, I didn't see any idols there.'

'Why should there be any? Idolatry is forbidden among the Sikhs just as it is among the Muslims.'

The fact was so new to me I had difficulty believing it. And although I didn't disagree with him, I concluded that surely he must be mistaken. From Katra Mahaan Singh we cut through Paathi Ground and came to the Gol Mosque of Sharifpura. Then we took a straight lane and soon found ourselves at the tracks in front of Ehsan's house. I should have turned towards my house after crossing Paathi Ground because my house was nearer to that, but four o'clock was still three hours away. Why be holed up in my house so soon? Why not spend some more time with Ehsan shooting the breeze? We climbed the stairs and went on to the rooftop. For sure it would be hot there, but it was also the only spot in the house where we could find the privacy we were seeking. We moved about aimlessly in the blazing sun, jumping up to spy on the neighbourhood through the peepholes in the wall which stood at about the height of a man along the edges of the roof. The nearby roofs were totally deserted, not a living soul anywhere in sight. Winding alleys, straight paths, whatever we saw was desolate. The ogre of sunlight had sucked life out of everything and put it to sleep. The dust-coated greenery of the parks was spread far and wide like a drab, green, stationary cloud, with a blue but equally dull sky resting over it like an overturned bowl. At the back of Ehsan's house a crow sat panting on a thick, white, misshapen limb of the scrawny peepal tree. It cawed a couple of times, and then, getting tired of its perch, flew off towards the drab green cloud. We couldn't bear the sun any longer. We went and sat under the cabin-like structure on the stairs. As we were quite tired, we leaned our backs against the wall, stretched out our legs, and perspired vigorously in silence. Ehsan started to sing softly:

Don't cry my heart, don't cry.
How may I comfort you . . .

He was singing so well that I gazed at his face in wonder. Unaffected, he went on. I thought I saw tears falling from his eyes. But how could I dare ask what was bothering him. Perhaps they weren't tears; perhaps they were only beads of perspiration. Had they been tears his voice might have choked. But he was still singing in a sorrowful voice. If they were really tears, he himself didn't know he was shedding them. After the song ended, he shut his eyes and sat quietly for a while. When he opened them, I thought they were brimming with moisture. Standing up I said, 'Okay, I'm leaving now.' He didn't say anything, just nodded once. On my way home a single thought occupied my mind: if he was crying, why was it? Was he thinking of his father's painful death? Had the circumstances of his family become unbearable? But neither of these had anything to do with the subject or the melody of the song. The next day I kept asking him but he just smiled and remained silent. Perhaps he himself didn't know that he had been crying. Today, fifty years later, one possible answer to the riddle comes to mind: perhaps even before seeing

Lali that day, he knew he was going to lose her and his utter helplessness in the matter had made him cry.

The third morning he stealthily came up the stairs to my room and whispered, 'I'll be down in the street. Come quickly.'

I was astounded to see him without his ubiquitous cap, in fact so astounded that I forgot my own annoyance with him and asked, 'What happened to your cap?'

We started off for his house, threading our way through the alleys and then along the tracks. A drumbeater in the street was announcing a blackout that evening from eight to ten. I said, 'Again? What a pain, yaar! You don't have to worry about this sort of thing. No civil defence man can come to your area. You can keep the lights on as long as you want.'

'There's a blackout at our house every night. Whether anyone comes there or not, the lantern is put out every night at eight, to save oil.'

'You pulled a nice one on me the other day. You slipped away before I could come.'

'When they passed by I waited for you for some time. But when you failed to show up, I went after them.'

'Whatever happened to your cap?'

'Lali made me stop wearing it. She asked me if I had seen anyone my age wearing a cap like that. She said it didn't look nice on me, that I should stop wearing it. How could I tell her that I wore it to honour the memory of Mustapha Kamal Pasha—the only Muslim general in contemporary times to have fought and won against the British. She wouldn't have grasped all that. And besides, she asked so lovingly that I couldn't very well refuse. When the hair starts growing in a few days I'll look okay.'

'So now you're going to flaunt English-style hair as well, eh? What happened to all your declarations?'

'The hair doesn't matter. The real issue is equality among human beings.'

'Two meetings with Lali and you've already made all human beings equal?'

'You're a little piqued, aren't you, yaar?'

'And you seem a little happier than one need be.' We both laughed.

'So what did you talk about the last two days?' I asked.

'Both days Lali didn't gather any coal. Toti did it alone. Lali had made herself so beautiful that she didn't even look at all like the old Lali. She was wearing different clothes and she had bangles up to her elbows. Wait till you see them. They should be along soon. Lali was asking about you. She said I should definitely bring you along today.'

'Oh, I see. That's why you took the trouble to show up so early this morning!'

When we reached the veranda of his house, we saw a very long train filled with white folks halting at the signal, right in front of us. The soldiers, miserable from the heat, were swarming out of the doors and windows of the third-class compartments in their shorts and vests—filthy-looking, terribly sweaty and coated with dust. As soon as the train came to a complete stop, armed Indian soldiers, with their rifles cocked, posted themselves in front of every door. I said, 'Even Indian soldiers don't look that wretched. For what crime are these English soldiers being punished so badly?'

'They're not English soldiers,' he said. 'They're Italian prisoners of war, rounded up by the English after Rommel's retreat in Egypt. Because they're white, the English are transferring them to some cooler hilly place in Dalhousie. They've built a POW camp there. At the station they'll hitch a second engine to the back of the train. Then the same train will pass in front of us on the Pathankot lines. Let's go watch them up close.'

Meanwhile a crowd of half-naked children had gathered on both sides of the train. They were making a terrible racket with their laughing and loud entreaties, and the prisoners were tossing packets of biscuits, chocolate and cigarettes towards them. Because of the guards the Italians couldn't step out of the train, nor could the children get close to it. When we got near the train a prisoner tossed a box of biscuits at us. We looked at it for a while. Then I said, 'Pick it up, yaar. It's a freebie.' Ehsan made a V sign with his fingers and held it up for the prisoner to see, saying to me, 'Watch how angry this makes him.' The Italian shook his finger to indicate denial, then he made the same V with his fingers pointing downwards. We played this game with the man for a bit and then returned to the veranda. I asked, 'Have you ever seen a real living Englishman?'

'Yes, once, but from a distance. My mother and I were returning after visiting Father. As I was trying to board the Frontier Mail at the Lahore station, I saw two Englishmen come out of the refreshments room and go into the air-conditioned compartment. A white soldier was moving people aside to make way for them on the platform. Then another time, an army special loaded with white soldiers stopped here for a second.'

I asked, 'Yaar, do you suppose they gave us biscuits because they think we're like the famine-stricken Bengalis?'

'Who knows? Maybe they did. Anyway, most Indians do

look starved. Did you read the news of the famine in the papers? Yaar, the British have treated the Bengalis very cruelly. Such harsh punishment for demanding independence! About a million have already perished. Only God knows how many more will follow them. Do you remember the pictures we saw at Cold Well?'

'Yes, I do. They sent a shudder through me.'

'They were nothing compared to the ones that are coming out now. You won't be able to eat the whole day if you so much as look at them—corpses lying about in the streets being torn up by dogs and crows. It tears my heart every time I read the stories that are printed. One woman had gathered a handful of rice for her children by walking up and down the road between the station and the rice warehouse the whole day. As she was returning home in the evening, another hungry man snatched it from her and ran away. The poor woman could do nothing but cry.'

'Then what happened?'

'Well, what always happens. She must have died, and the children must have died too.'

'Isn't anybody doing anything for the Bengalis?'

'As a matter of fact, grain is being shipped to Calcutta from this part of the country on the freight trains, and I myself have seen such trains passing by here. But whether the government over there can manage to get it to the needy is something else again.'

Talk of famine put us in a gloomy mood and we sat staring at the tracks in awkward silence. After the train transporting the Italian prisoners had moved on, the Frontier Mail went clattering by on the same tracks, stirring up the dust as well as the empty biscuit boxes and chocolate wrappers which began to dance about in the air. The biscuits that I had eaten made me belch loudly and I felt strangely embarrassed.

The Frontier Mail had come and gone and still there was no sign of Lali and Toti. Ehsan seemed visibly worried. 'Let's go take a look by their tents,' he said. 'I hope they haven't decamped and moved on.'

'If their men find out about us they'll beat us up.'

'We'll just look from a distance. It isn't far from here either, we only need to go up to the bend where the road to Ambala forks off.'

We reached the gypsies' encampment, winding our way through the orchards. It was deserted. Only ashes swirled about in a dozen or so hearths that had been fashioned by slapping a bunch of bricks together, and donkey droppings were lying about here and there. A strange melancholy feeling, a sinister desolation pervaded the whole site. The tribe had apparently packed up and moved sometime during the night. When we returned, Ehsan went up the stairs. I was called over by his mother. 'Eh Saeed, did you ever give your father my message about the permit?' Instead of replying, I just stood there staring at the ground.

Safia said, 'Aapa, he's too scared of his father. He wouldn't have had the spunk to talk. Everybody is afraid of him. He's so irritable.'

'Son, if you had told me that I would've tried to find another way. But here I was sitting and waiting for the permit to arrive. There's nothing to buy in the market: rice, cloth, sugar, kerosene, you name it. And we can't afford the black-market prices. Here we don't even have electricity. A canister of kerosene could've given us a little bit of comfort for a few days. Things weren't all that bad before, but the damned war—it's ruined everything. God's curse on it. It shows no signs of ending. Four years and it's still raging on.'

I went upstairs. Ehsan was sitting on a cot near the covered part of the stairs, sunk in deep thought. In the blue sky, a bevy of kites flew about in a circle above our heads. Dark clouds were advancing from the northeast. A whiff of cool air hit my face and hair. I sat down beside him. Lali and Toti's departure hadn't affected me at all, but Ehsan had taken it hard. Looking back, it seems that Lali had etched the pink line of romance a shade too deeply on Ehsan's impressionable heart. After some time I said, 'It's going to rain. I'll leave now.'

'Fine.'

As I stepped out of the vestibule, I saw a young Sikh standing in the lane holding on to a bicycle. 'Is this Farman sahib's house?' he asked.

'Yes, it is,' I said.

'If his mother is in, please, I'd like to speak to her.'

When I went inside to tell her, both the mother and daughter gasped together, 'God have mercy!' Aapa carefully covered her head with her dupatta, walked over to the door and asked from behind it, 'Yes, son, what's the matter?'

'Maa-ji, I work with Farman at the factory. Today around ten in the morning, the Putli Ghar police came to the factory and took him away. Farman made a speech in a meeting of the Putli Ghar handloom workers five or six days ago. The police claim that he incited the workers to destroy property and assault the owners. But don't worry, it's not a serious case. He'll be out soon on bail. The party is working on it. I'll bring you his salary for the current month. And this, here, is his bicycle. Please take it.'

I moved forward and took the bicycle.

Aapa said, 'Son, such lawsuits are nothing new for us. Those who care for others must face them. Why worry, God will look after us. But thank you for coming and letting us know.'

Holding the bicycle aloft, I walked up the four steps into the vestibule where I found Aapa leaning against the wall and Safia, her eyes filled with tears, offering her a bowl of water. Aapa had turned pale and was perspiring profusely. Supporting herself on Safia, she lumbered into the courtyard and sat down on a cot, holding her head in her hands. She seemed to be saying to herself: the same old cycle has started again. Oh, how I wish it hadn't. I don't have the strength to take it any more.

Safia sat beside her quietly, shedding tears and massaging her shoulders. Aapa opened her eyes and said to me, 'Go get Ehsan,' and then to Safia, 'You can be sure the police will raid the house by tonight, if not sooner. Put all of Farman's papers and files in a sack and give it to Ehsan. Tell him to take it to Mamun's house right this minute. Tomorrow we'll look for a safer place. And all those posters and party papers lying behind the stairs, take them to the backyard and burn them.'

When Ehsan came down she told him, 'Safia will give you a sack of papers. Take it to Mamun's house and then go to Lala Krishan Lal's office and ask him to apply to the magistrate for Farman's bail.'

Ehsan said, 'But the Lala's been behind bars himself for a while now.'

She fell to thinking and then said, 'In that case, go to Saeed's father at the courthouse and ask him to find a lawyer to arrange for the bail. And tell him that I'll be coming to see him this evening. We must also arrange for somebody to post the bail if it's granted.'

In the evening Ehsan's mother came to our house with Safia in tow to talk to my father about Farman's lawsuit and to ask him to find a guarantor. I was afraid my father would give them a piece of his mind, but he surprised me. Not only did he listen to them patiently, he also assured them pleasantly enough of help, conducting himself with exceeding politeness throughout the conversation. And my mother, in a rare gesture of hospitality, instantly dispatched me to Maulvi Daoud's for some sandalwood sharbat which she then offered to the guests. I had often heard my father make incredibly scathing and hateful remarks about this family. If I was now having difficulty figuring him out, it would have been even more difficult for Ehsan's mother and Safia to guess his true feelings about them. Later on he did a lot of running about for Farman's bail and even got them the permit from the Civil Supplies Department. All this was far too confusing for me. If he hated them so much, what could explain this immense compassion and show of warmth now? Why display so much courtesy in their presence and so much hatred behind their backs?

After they had thrashed out every aspect of Farman's case, my mother, as if to carry on with the conversation, broached a new subject. 'Aapa,' she said, 'shouldn't you also be thinking about Safia's marriage now?' Hearing that, Safia got up and went into the other room to be with my sisters.

'Beti, I *am*—day and night. My brother has asked for her hand for his son Mahmood. Farman is opposed to the match, but I have said yes. True, the man who had promised to fight for India's freedom laid down his life in order to remain loyal to that promise. But this doesn't obligate me—does it?—that I should ruin the life of a simple stay-at-home girl for the sake of India's freedom? First she gets fired from her job—why? Because her father was a Congressite. And now I shouldn't marry her off because the young man serves in the British army. Doesn't that amount to a double punishment for the poor girl? Let Mahmood come back home on his next vacation. I'll get her married, whether Farman agrees or not, and I'll send her off, if it comes to that, in the very clothes she has on.'

Straightforward and pure-hearted, Ehsan's mother was one of those rare people whose tongues said only what lay in their hearts, who met life's problems head-on and dealt with them regardless of their severity. They always met a person, no matter how wicked or ill intentioned, with an open heart, and didn't leave a back door open to escape through when things got tough.

Farman's arrest did a lot of damage to me personally. My secret was out. My parents knew right away that even though Ehsan didn't come to our place any more, I, nonetheless, visited him every day. I was sure I was going to get it the minute Ehsan's family left. But I was absolutely bowled over when Father demonstrated unusual forbearance at my blatant disobedience of his order. He admonished me, but mildly, giving the same advice much more gently which he had meted out very sternly before.

'Son, we tell you this for your own good,' he said, 'not because we've got a grudge against Ehsan. But, let's face it, he's very irresponsible and he's a drifter. He's already failed three times in school. And besides, he takes after his father and brother in temperament. He isn't afraid of getting into trouble himself, so why would he care if he dragged you into it as well? Take this court case, for example. Farman brought it on himself. Would you call it a wise move? There is hardly any food in the house and he goes about making speeches to rouse the workers. He knows full well that without his salary everybody in the house will starve. But did he consider that? No, not for a minute. He just went ahead and spat everything out. They're all like that, except Aapa. That poor woman has spent her entire life fighting all alone battles that they had started. Brother Bashir Ahmad did it, and now Farman is following in his footsteps. Tomorrow Ehsan will do the same. A streak of insanity runs through all of them. It can't help but show itself.'

My mother interrupted, 'Sons take after their fathers. It's your family, after all. As for Aapa, an outsider, the poor woman just got trapped.'

'Precisely why I keep telling your son to stay away from Ehsan. I know he has the same streak in him. I had it too; in fact I still do. Many times I think of doing something wild.' He laughed and looked at Mother expecting approbation, adding, 'At least they had a haveli which they could sell to make ends meet. We don't even have a house of our own. But it has to be granted that Aapa is a very brave woman. She has never asked anyone for help and has dealt with her monumental problems very discreetly. No matter what, she kept in touch with all her relatives, shared in their joys and sorrows, and never tried to blame anyone else for her misfortunes. Now Safia is to be married to someone whom even many big shots would die to have as a son-in-law. The boy is a captain in the army. Must be getting around fifteen hundred rupees. Are you listening? Fifteen hundred rupees a month! My whole ten months' salary barely amounts to that much.'

My mother butted in, 'Yes, the good Lord has rewarded Aapa for her patience. Finally her wishes are granted. That's right, God may take a long time, but He's not blind. He does reward.'

'And Farman, my own blood, my own nephew, what does he say? "Tell them no. We don't want this match." Just look at him! That's why I say all three have their heads screwed on backwards. They're complete idiots.'

A few days later I discovered that my father had decided to pull me out of Muslim School and enrol me in a Government School at the end of the holidays so that I might be rescued from Ehsan's company. My father succeeded in his plans, to the extent that the switch pretty much ended my association with Ehsan. Whether this change had any positive effect on my academic performance or on the formation of my character is debatable. I was given to wandering by nature and it didn't take me long to seek out my own kind at the new school. Some of them were Hindu and Sikh boys. The company of new friends introduced me to new types of vagrancy. Since this school was far from my home, a bicycle was purchased for me. First the range of my vagrancy widened and then, because of the sudden onset of a change in my temperament, my preferences also evolved. The nature of vagrancy itself changed with these circumstances. We started smoking, but only now and then. In time it was the incurable addiction of the movies that got the better of us.

I seemed to be in a big hurry to grow up, all because this would make the girls take notice of me. It pained me to look at myself in the mirror and find that my face still showed no sign of a growing moustache, and that the soft greenish down on my upper lip was still there. To tell the truth, even smoking was taken up in order to parade around as a grown-up. A dark moss had begun to grow on Ehsan's cheeks and upper lip, but that fool wouldn't even start shaving. Perhaps he was thinking of wearing a beard. He still came to see me, secretly, every ten or fifteen days. In the beginning we even went out together for a stroll, but now I'd soon tire of his company. It seemed we no longer shared anything in common. I began to wonder whether there was any point in my continuing to see him, especially when his presence became a source not of pride but of embarrassment for me before my fashionable and relatively well-to-do friends. One time when I was forced to introduce him to my friends, they simply didn't take any notice of him, and it was obvious that he wasn't feeling comfortable in their company either. He soon left my room. After he was gone, Madan asked, 'Yaar, who is he, this uncle-ish character?' All three of them chuckled. I admitted in a rather hushed tone that he was a distant relative. The matter came to rest there.

After Rommel's retreat the African front came firmly and completely under Allied control and the theatre of action shifted to Europe, where the rest of the war would be staged. In the Far East, not only had the Japanese advance been halted, the Allies also took back some of the islands the Japanese had seized earlier. I don't know whether it was because of the war, or Aapa's counselling, or the shock he must have felt when, feeling ashamed of my parents' attitude towards him, I told him the real reason why I had to change schools, but Ehsan definitely took a second look at his academic plans. When I graduated to the ninth grade, he made it there too. It wasn't long after the beginning of classes when Farman was given a six-month sentence. Ehsan was forced to quit school and take up a job as a salesman with some Muslim shoe-seller in Katra Jaimal Singh. By the time Farman was released and could find another job, I was already in the tenth grade. After wasting another year, Ehsan once again enrolled in the ninth grade at Muslim School. He spent much of his free time in the neighbourhood reading room on the main street square. Mornings, he read the Urdu newspapers published from Lahore and looked at the pictures in the *Tribune*. He returned in the evening to look at the pictures in the English newspapers from Delhi and Calcutta. However, these evening visits were terminated during his employment at the shoe shop because he got off from work quite late. The small shopkeepers around the reading room addressed him as Bao Ehsan and accorded him a respectful place in their midst. Wherever he sat down, a gaping throng of tonga drivers, pushcart salesmen and other people from the working class, besides the neighbouring shop owners, surrounded him, and equipped with the fresh information received from him, made unsuccessful attempts to peer into their futures. When they found nothing there, they commented with an air of resignation: 'Governments change every day. What difference does it make to us? We'll always remain down and out, always toiling to scrape up enough to put two square meals a day on the table for our families.'

After the slaughter of the Khaksars, no new Muslim movement had emerged. The demand for Pakistan hadn't picked up momentum yet. At most it was a battle cry whose political value amounted to no more than a vague threat. While politically the Muslims flaunted an attitude of indifference and devil-may-care, inwardly they couldn't have been more rattled or agitated. And in this district with a hundred per cent Muslim population, Ehsan, clad in his pyjama-kurta made of coarse homespun cotton, laid out before the masses, in great detail and with compelling argument, the Congress position—namely, freedom for India and the absolute necessity of revolution—and vehemently opposed the establishment of Pakistan. His audience heard him and dismissed him, though scarcely anybody actually opened their mouths. Once in a great while one of them would express his doubts, muttering under his breath, 'Well, why then is the Congress party crowded with Hindus? Surely they must see some advantage in joining it. Why else this scramble?' Then the doubter would be overtaken by despair, 'The English will never let go of India, nor will India ever gain independence. Things are going to go on and on like this. But at least Jinnah does talk about the Muslims.' Unable to stomach this praise of Jinnah, a tonga driver, who had perhaps spent some time in the company of Ahrars and Khaksars, started telling story after story about how the top leadership of the Muslim League was hopelessly westernized and cherished the English. Ehsan described in detail the views of the Muslim ulema and the popularity the Congress enjoyed among the Muslims of the North West Frontier Province. All this back and forth produced the same result it always had: people who had come there to find some way out of their confusion left even more confounded than before. The Hindus had embraced India's freedom as their sole, distinct, clear and definite political objective. Muslims, on the other hand, didn't have the foggiest idea what they wanted or who to turn to for leadership. To them every political solution seemed like the proverbial 'out of the frying pan into the fire'. At most they would think about one thing: if only the good old days of the Khilafat-e Rashida could somehow return. How to live in today's world, and what its demands were going to be, was something nobody paid any attention to, nor even had the ability to grasp.

In the past Parveen had seemed to be a rather unremarkable girl, but by the time she reached the tenth grade she had turned into quite an attractive young lady, tall, graceful and glowing. Her sallow complexion had, as it were, become burnished, and her liquid black eyes had taken on the same winsome, endearing quality as a doe's. In my own mind, I had fallen head over heels in love with her like some fairy-tale prince, with union or death being the only options left. The reality was that we were only playing at the game of love. As a little girl she had played with her toy dolls; now she was through playing with those. She had become a doll herself and turned me into one as well. Our love amounted to no more than smiling and casting loving glances at each other as we stood face-to-face at the windows. We still hadn't gotten the nerve to go beyond that. But this became quite a diversion for my classmates, Aslam, Mushtaq, Madan and Rajinder, who visited my house quite often. They lost no time in dubbing her Laila and me—a fairly heavyset boy—Majnun. No matter what the conversation was about, they would find a way to slip in a reference to Laila–Majnun, obliquely if not expressly. To say something witty with a double meaning, or to say something indirect with just the right amount of humour is not everybody's cup of tea. But, although their simpering attempts often yielded nothing more than meaningless or inane comments, I nonetheless enjoyed their joking quite a bit, and never wanted them to quit the subject. Every one of their remarks smacked of envy or jealousy, which I found quite comforting. And besides, no matter what they said, it made me feel a tinge of pride—a pride that gave me a strange sense of achievement. Gradually these incidentals came to have greater importance for me than Parveen's love, which had been the cause of it all.

Mushtaq's father had retired as a deputy superintendent of Police. In those days such jobs were generally reserved for the English and rarely fell to the lot of an Indian. Aslam's father was a doctor—a specialist in what was, back then, the incurable and fatal disease of tuberculosis—and was raking in money with both hands. Madan's father had been given the title of Rai Bahadur by the English and was a sessions judge. Rajinder was the son of a rich contractor. I wasn't someone of their class, but I was dying to be counted as one. My room was the hangout where they all gathered to escape from the peace and ordered neatness of their own bungalows and to have a taste of freedom, or to smoke or to just shoot the breeze. There were no servants here who would report to their mothers on their sons' activities and their acquaintances. We would roll around like dirt-covered donkeys on the matted floor, turn somersaults, or tangle with each other like wrestlers. Here there was no fear of breaking anything or messing up the décor. We would openly indulge in obscenities and tell dirty jokes with perfect ease. My parents never imposed any restrictions on their visiting me, perhaps because they mistakenly assumed their son was befriending the children of the beau monde. They didn't know that friendships only thrive among equals, friendships with those higher or lower than oneself inevitably become self-effacing or patronizing after a time. We mostly talked about movies and movie stars, or else we tried to gauge the beauty of the daughters of the city's rich and famous from the scandals circulating about them. Sometimes, in order to show the superiority of the lifestyles of their families over others, my friends would describe their trips to different hill stations or their visits to posh hotels. Or they would talk about the styles, cuts and colours of their clothing and the specific occasions and times when it was appropriate to wear this or that, or about their pride in owning, or their regret over not owning, some rare breed of dog or the choicest brands of automobiles, watches or radios. In short, their speech never failed to communicate a sense of arrogance about what they did possess, or of wistful longing for certain material comforts or bodily pleasures that had eluded them thus far. When their conversations went far beyond my social position or financial means, I would tire of my flights of fancy and drop down to the mundane reality of facts. I would wonder then whether genuine expressions of compassion for suffering humanity had departed from my life along with Ehsan. Slavery, backwardness, misfortune and famine—these were not the issues that occupied our minds. And yet Rajinder's and Madan's sympathies lay with the Congress even though, unlike many other Hindus, they neither wore homespun cotton, nor served the Congress in any way. They did respect Gandhi and Nehru though. When I told them the story of Ehsan's father, they listened closely to each detail, speechless with wonder and reverence. Afterwards, whenever they had occasion to meet Ehsan, they visibly treated him with honour and due appreciation. Mushtaq and Aslam, on the other hand, remained totally unaffected by the story of Ehsan's father's martyrdom for the country and the resulting misfortunes of his family.

My friendship with these four lasted about two or two and

a half years. In any case, it wouldn't have continued beyond the matriculation exams since they all had resolved to go to Lahore for their first year of college, while I was destined to enrol in a local college. However, the occurrence of two events in quick succession pretty much ended our friendship even before the exams. Madan's sister was getting married in January. He invited the other three but ignored me altogether. This prejudicial treatment shocked and tormented me. For the first time in my life, a strange sense of my own lowliness and a feeling of disgrace gripped me. I felt like a fool, cut off from everybody, alone, utterly alone. I couldn't figure out what had happened to me. I couldn't have been excluded because I was a Muslim; two of the others were also Muslims. I had never been to Madan's home, so none of my actions could possibly have offended his parents. I didn't shed any tears, but my heart was crying out. Again and again I was reminded of Ehsan who had always been treated this way by my parents. Eventually I found out that my suspicions were justified. Madan's parents had refused to invite me because of my father's lower social status. So, I was not one of them. I was whatever my father's and my social status implied. Friendship was a meaningless thing. The real thing was class. A crow doesn't become a peacock by sticking a few peacock feathers in its tail.

After that, Madan, out of embarrassment, never came to my house, but the other three did drop by now and then. As usual, I accompanied them to movies or on bicycle rides through Company Bagh, but my heart—now that I had been made conscious of my true worth—was bereft of the love I had felt for them earlier.

It was a very pleasant evening in mid-February. A touch

of spring had animated the weather. A clean, cool breeze was blowing playfully around us, stirring up joy in our hearts and refreshing our bodies. We decided to park our bicycles on Lawrence Road and walk as far as we could along the Mall. Since Aslam had to leave early and we were, at any rate, heading in the direction of his home, he hung on to his bicycle. Walking leisurely, taking in the pleasurable weather, we came up to the Lawrence Road intersection and went along on the sidewalk of the quiet and peaceful Mall, going in the opposite direction from Cold Well. Colonial-style houses stood in all their majesty and grandeur on both sides for a distance of about ten kanals. (How could the English, who had built such bungalows, ever have left India easily?) We started playing a game, flicking our cigarette butts. We would hold them between the thumb and middle finger and then strike them with the forefinger to see how far they would fly. The milky white light falling from the electric poles on either side of the street had become stronger with the deepening evening shadows, so visibility had shrunk down to the light bulbs themselves, along with the twelve-foot-wide street and the two-and-a-half-foot-tall sinthiya hedge illumined by them. Everything else had vanished. Once in a while a cook or a waiter passed us on his bicycle, or a slow-paced tonga lazily plodded along. We left the sidewalk and started walking on the street. When I flicked a cigarette butt, it went sliding along the road, turning a few somersaults and throwing off sparks along the way, before it became caught in the base of the hedge on the other side. Although in terms of the distance covered my cigarette butt was second to Mushtaq's, which had gone straight across the hedge, mine had put up a fine display of fireworks in the street that we all enjoyed heartily.

Meanwhile we saw three girls coming up ahead some hundred yards away. They were talking and giggling among themselves, moving their bodies flirtatiously. Rajinder suggested that I light a cigarette immediately, and when we had come alongside the girls, I should repeat my earlier performance, but this time make the butt stop right in front of their feet. It would be fun to watch them jump up in fright. Considering myself an expert in cigarette flipping, I got ready. The girls, all three of them, were pretty. The effort they had put into their make-up and outfits made it obvious they were headed to some party. Especially the girl in the middle, she looked exceptionally beautiful in a sparkling white silk sari with a low-cut matching blouse. She seemed like some fairy who had come down from the sky for a stroll and who would soon fly back. They were entirely engrossed in their own conversation, totally oblivious to our presence. When we got near them I ejected the cigarette butt, but instead of gliding along the surface of the road it flew straight up and went towards them like a rocket. I was scared that it might fall on one of their heads and God knows what damage that would do.

Too late now, the arrow had already left the bow. I had a faint hope that it would land on the opposite sidewalk instead and I would be spared embarrassment and regret. But it went straight into the blouse of the girl in the middle. She didn't scream, only started hissing and shifting her weight from foot to foot fretfully because of the sensation of being burned. The other girls tried, one after the other and without success, to stick their fingers inside her blouse and remove the offender. Aslam immediately took off on his bicycle. The rest of us stood facing the girls feeling contrite and wanting to help, but unable to do so. Lord knows how, but within just a short time a crowd of people gathered on this otherwise deserted street, everyone wanting to know what had happened. In the meantime four boys, quite a bit older than us, happened to come by on a couple of bicycles. Taking full advantage of the situation, they tried to establish themselves as the heroes. First they politely asked the girls what had happened. When the girls didn't answer, they turned towards us. 'You must have done something. Come on, out with it!' By then the girls had somehow managed to extricate the remains of the burning cigarette, and hurried on without a word.

I breathed a sigh of relief. We would deal with what was to come next. At least the poor girl was out of the misery I had brought upon her. The boys, who had depicted themselves as full of grief and anger in front of the girls, were now bending over with laughter. One of them addressed us, 'Bravo! Whichever one of you did that is a remarkable marksman.' Afraid that the girls' real guardians would come after us, we took to our heels. But luckily no one came.

We assumed the matter was over and done with. But, despite his swift retreat, the girls had recognized Aslam because he lived in their neighbourhood. And through him we too were discovered. Before long, news of the incident, with all its details, made it to the homes of Mushtaq and Rajinder, who put the blame squarely on me. The girls' families didn't confront my father about the matter, probably because in such delicate situations, where one's girls are involved, the exchange of words with one's inferiors can only bring more disgrace. Only Rajinder's father complained to the headmaster, in a private letter, that there were goons like

Saeed in his school who incited their relatively innocent children to commit such horrible and dangerous mischief, and that it was his duty to reprimand and discipline such individuals, etc., etc. It was my good fortune that within a few days the tenth graders were going to be excused from attending classes in order to prepare for their exams. The headmaster only summoned me and gave me a stern rebuke. Mercifully, he let me go and also didn't summon my father. That incident pretty much ended my friends' visits to my place and our going around together.

As long as the war continued, it seemed not to be taking place on earth but on some other planet. Although it didn't concern anybody here, its effects were, of course, painfully noticeable in the scarcity of consumer goods and the exorbitant prices. Once in a while we also had to suffer the inconvenience of blackouts. Every third month or so mock exercises were conducted to drill the public in air-raid defence. The siren would be sounded and the police would run frantically to chase people out of the streets as they stood making fun of the mock air raids. Without the willing cooperation of the public, a large-scale drama such as that can't be staged successfully. The whole project becomes as ridiculous as trying to weigh a frog in a balance. During the entire war, no one had even heard gunfire, let alone a bomb explode. Although the world's most devastating war was being fought and hundreds of thousands were perishing, for our people it had no more significance than a game because it wasn't our war. My insensitive friends suspected that the sole purpose of the war was to deprive them, from the day they attained consciousness to their last dying breath, of Chinese garments of the finest silk and high-quality English suits. They were convinced that the war was not going to end before doomsday, and it pained them that their parents had enjoyed all the rare things in life whereas they themselves had been denied.

Whenever Ehsan came to visit me, he would take me aside and advise me never to try to befriend Parveen, that such things in one's own neighbourhood amounted to folly, and that if I was, nonetheless, genuinely interested in her, she should be told never to show herself at the window when my friends were around. How could I tolerate such an affront to my honour—her showing herself to others so openly? But, of course, that advice went the way all such advice goes. It was heard but conveniently ignored. In fact, that Parveen didn't show herself at the window when my friends were around was precisely their complaint against her. The attachment I felt for her, which even I, in those days, took to be genuine love, was less that and more a form of self-conceit. Why, she must have appeared to them to be an equal of Sassi and Sohni after the fabricated and much embellished stories I had told them of my meetings with her. My good fortune made their breasts burn with jealousy, so much so that the merest spray of water would have made them hiss with a burst of steam. One time they became so enflamed with a longing to catch a glimpse of her that they skipped school with me and stood waiting in the street to her school for hours in the unforgiving sun. Her beauty pained their hearts even more, and when she looked at me with a tender smile, they were almost toasted. I felt like I was in seventh heaven. Compared to brats brought up in the streets, the ones raised in the loneliness of bungalows, under their parents' watchful gaze, tended to be really quite naive and innocent because they faced the realities of life much later.

As soon as the war ended, it seemed as if an electric current passed through India's political climate. The atmosphere became more strained and tense by the day, and people, although not knowing exactly, felt in their bones that something was going to happen. But what? It was impossible to divine. Even the most astute political leaders were unable to say just what might emerge from the shadows of the future. Heated discussions erupted among people in the streets and bazaars. Speculation was rife, and so were open displays of hopeless sentimentality and maudlin self-pity, without any sense of decorum, and all done on social and particularly religious grounds with generous references to history. During the time when the Muslim League became a household word among Muslims and the cry for Pakistan was raised, my father, like most Muslims, became a staunch supporter of Pakistan. Every evening after supper, the elders and notables of our street would perch on the raised porches outside our homes and discuss politics. Young men and boys could sit there, but they weren't permitted to express their opinions. To those who opposed the creation of Pakistan, my father would say, 'Is there anyone who knows the Congress better than we do? Didn't we nourish its foundations with our blood? Why, my own elder brother, he died in jail for the sake of the Congress, writhing in pain, racked by tuberculosis. But now we can see through Gandhi and Nehru's bigotry and the Hindus' relentless and eternal prejudice against Muslims. And this prejudice is not going to disappear. Indian Muslims have been forced to demand a separate homeland for their own survival. This is the only solution now.'

He would be asked, 'And what about the Muslims who

would be left behind in India? Who would guarantee their safety?'

'Why, the Hindus who would be left behind in Pakistan,' he'd answer.

Even the leaders could not have guessed then that there would be a transfer of population, and on such a massive scale at that, on the basis of religion. Later on, at the time of Partition, the blood of the innocents that was shed in the Punjab could not be matched for a comparable area even by the bloodiest war in the history of mankind.

Maulvi Karam Din said, 'Brother, bartered marriages, as anybody knows, just don't work. How do you suppose two hostile nations and races can be trusted with the safety of their minorities on the basis of barter?'

In the two years preceding Partition, when the idea of Pakistan had become a watchword in just about every household, and when every child was yelling out 'Pakistan Zindabad' in a frenzy, critics like Maulvi Karam Din were struck dumb and clammed up in fear for their lives. In the tempest of emotions all reasoning and logic was swept away like so much straw. Ehsan would come especially to tell me, 'Don't be misled by all this noise and tumult. This is nothing but the crafty handiwork of the British. When they saw India slipping out of their hands, they decided to break it into bits so that it would never emerge as a world power. Watch it! Lest you become a partner in this crime by siding with the Muslim League.'

What I say now goes back to the time after the establishment of Pakistan. My father's petition for an evacuee property was turned down by the claims officer for some reason. I was with my father. He raised such a fuss over this that I became very upset. He was describing his disagreements with Maulvi Karam Din on the porch in the street outside as the 'ideological battles we fought in every street and alleyway with the enemies of the Muslim League and Pakistan'.

When I was in college, Muslim students staged a demonstration in the Hall Bazaar against the government of Khizr Hayat in the Punjab. Ninety per cent of the police consisted of Muslims, who had, by then, switched their sympathies to the Muslim League. They engaged in a very mild—indeed loving—clubbing of the demonstrators. A club hit me on the thigh. Because I was at the head of the demonstration, I was whisked away to the police station. I sat there for about three hours along with the other students who had been picked up. There they served us a cooled sweet sharbat to drink and other goodies. By evening I was home. That incident my father now blew up into: 'We suffered beatings by the police for the sake of Pakistan. We were dragged through the streets. We were incarcerated. Our brothers and sisters were cut to pieces in the riots. Our houses were torched. Our property was looted. Is this how you reward us for all our sacrifices?' The officer-in-charge panicked and accepted my father's claim as submitted. My father kissed the officer's hands in gratitude and came out.

It was inevitable that this continual incitement to hatred should erupt in the worst kind of riots. People who had not so much as heard a shot fired during the entire war were now frantically grabbing their daggers and kirpans and cutting up innocent human beings to claim their share in perpetrating violence. The individual had disappeared in the aggregate of his fellow-believers. A single unit didn't count—it could be severed and dumped with impunity; the collective entity was all that mattered. The numbers of the enemy slain versus those of one's own faith were touted proudly like cricket match scores.

Once started, the riots continued sporadically until after Independence Day on 15 August. On that day we sat barricaded behind the tall iron gates of our neighbourhood. About a month earlier, Ehsan and his family had abandoned their unprotected house in the open area and moved into Sharifpura. There too the gates stayed closed at all times. Permission from four guards had to be obtained before one could visit another quarter. The guard of one neighbourhood would call out loudly to his counterpart in the other asking whether such-and-such person could come across. The other would respond in the affirmative. Only then would the person concerned dash across the street dividing the two residential areas—a street that at one time had buzzed with life, but was now completely deserted—and go into the intended neighbourhood. Unless absolutely essential, such back-and-forth movement was discouraged. Ehsan's mamun felt compelled to leave his home in the inner city and seek refuge with some relatives in Sharifpura. The collective resistance of the Muslims had pretty much ended in this Hindu-majority city, and the entire Muslim population had moved to these two neighbourhoods for safety, at times as many as six families piling into a single house. Even the air was becoming insufficient, let alone food. It started to stink everywhere. After two hundred and fifty years of bondage to the English, an independent India had come into being. Pakistan had been formed a day earlier. The defeated Muslims of this city looked heartbroken, their faces pale, their eyes downcast, in mortal fear of an attack any minute, which, fortunately, didn't materialize. It didn't materialize because the Hindus and Sikhs suspected that the Muslims had a lot of manpower and stockpiles of weapons. Finally, the Muslims were able to board trains which stopped near their respective neighbourhoods and make their way safely to Pakistan.

A year and a half before that, Safia and Mahmood had been married and we all had had great fun participating in the wedding. Now, on the first morning of independent India, Mahmood, outfitted in his army uniform and accompanied by six soldiers from the Baluch regiment, pulled his army truck into the street facing our lane. After identifying himself to the guards at the gates, he came to us and told my father that he had first gone to his own house in the inner city and had found it razed to the ground, the cinders still glowing like charcoal embers in an oven. Only the back wall, blackened by smoke, still held its ground, standing tall and unyielding. He didn't have time or he would have knocked that down too. He had just picked a burning coal from the ashes of his ancestral home, lit a cigarette, and walked away to Ehsan's house. He saw a Sikh's dead body lying prone beside the railroad tracks, with his bicycle lying close by. Ehsan's house was locked up. That gave him hope—perhaps they were alive. Earlier, the sight of his charred ancestral home had made him weep for his sisters and parents.

'There's no cause for alarm,' my father said. 'They're alive and well and at Abdul Latif's house in Sharifpura.'

At breakfast Mahmood said, 'All the houses in Ehsan's area were locked up. Dogs were roaming the streets and the stench from the corpse wafted everywhere. It was quiet, terrifyingly quiet. Suddenly a flock of parrots took flight from a mango tree and went screeching over my head.' He laughed. 'My hand immediately went for my pistol. I thought the enemy had done something. But the Sikh lay there, as dead as ever.'

I wanted to ask him whether the parrot that had once turned around in flight to look at me and laugh was in that flock. Then I thought, who knows, it might've flown over to Pakistan already.

'Were Brother Bashir Ahmad alive today,' my father said, 'how incredibly happy he would have been to see his efforts finally bearing fruit. He'd have found a good position in the Congress government and something might have also trickled down to people like us.'

'But, Uncle,' Mahmood said, 'I can tell you on the basis of information received from the headquarters that not a single Muslim Congressite in the Punjab has been spared from suffering at the hands of the Hindu rioters. Some had their houses looted or razed, and some have even been killed. What protection did Phoophi and her family receive anyway?'

Because it was closed on all sides and the number of residents had increased sixfold, there was a crush of people in the narrow lanes of our neighbourhood at all times. People sat on cots or terraces or on the ground, quiet, subdued, waiting for death, staring at each other with dazed, fearful eyes. Someone, as if talking to himself, would whisper in the other's ear, 'Brother, what will happen now?'

'The same thing that will happen to everybody else. Don't worry. By the grace of God, everything will turn out okay.'

Five minutes later, this other person, in order to hear the same answer from the first one, would ask, 'Brother, what will happen now?' And the first man would recite the same formulaic answer. Bands of terrified children roamed about the streets all day long. No one even dared to talk loudly, much less get into mischief.

When Mahmood was done eating his breakfast, my father asked him very humbly, 'If there's room in the truck, please take us along.'

'Fine,' he said. 'But absolutely no baggage.'

'The hell with the baggage. We're lucky to get away with our lives. You've been like an angel of mercy for us.'

'Let's leave here together. We'll go to Sharifpura, pick up the others and then head off to Lahore.'

After it was decided to leave for Lahore, I ran to my room to change my shoes. Across the way Parveen stood at her window, her hair dishevelled, her clothes crumpled, her face distraught, and yet she appeared even more becoming. The news of our departure for Pakistan had swept across the whole neighbourhood the minute Mahmood showed up, and she too had heard it. A curious smile flashed across her face for a second and then died away—a smile entirely free of grief, remorse or complaint. I have tried to explain it to myself in a hundred different ways since then, but to no avail. I was still standing there facing her when she gently bolted the window shut. Her eyes were devoid of all expression.

When we came out of the house a crowd of thousands stood waiting, taking Mahmood to be the saviour. Everyone began asking, 'What will become of us? When will we be taken to Pakistan? What lies in store for us?' Mahmood stood up on an elevated front porch, picked one person in the crowd, and asked, 'All right, what do you want to know? The rest of you please keep quiet.'

The man said, 'There are thousands of Muslims in these

two neighbourhoods. What's being done for their safety? How will they get to Pakistan and when?'

'Frankly, I don't know,' Mahmood said. 'And neither does anybody else for that matter. I've barely been able to arrange for a truck to take my parents and some relatives to Pakistan. No plans have been made for your evacuation so far. It's a situation of total chaos. The number of army personnel we have is extremely limited. Since no one had imagined that the transfer of such a huge bulk of the population would be required, no plans or schemes were drawn up. We rush to wherever we sense greater danger. I'm sorry, I can't give you any immediate help. However, I do promise to communicate your concern to the headquarters. God willing, something will be done soon. For now you will have to depend upon your own resources to ensure your security.'

Faces, animated by a ray of hope a moment ago, wilted again. Many people made personal requests that he take their ailing mothers, or daughters, or themselves along, but Mahmood gently made them understand that there was really no room in the truck.

As we headed for the truck, so many people stood watching us wistfully that it was impossible to make our way through. Mahmood was walking ahead, then came my father, who was shaking hands with the people following him. After my father came my mother, with a small pouch of jewellery tucked under her arm, then my two sisters, and last of all, me. Before stepping out of the gate I turned around to look. Parveen's window was shut. From inside the high truck, I stood up to look again. It was still closed. Perhaps she had also shut the window of her heart on me—forever.

But the curious thing was that the window of my own heart, which didn't seem open earlier, burst wide open as though hit by a strong gust of wind. Forty years have passed, and it is still open, but she hasn't turned up, nor have I ever heard any news of her.

*

When I went to see Ehsan, I thought that he must be lying in bed moaning and wailing, vials of medicine lined up on the bedside table. After all, he had gone through a major surgery. I was still climbing the stairs when I heard, instead, the sound of his boisterous laughter. 'I'll be darned—he's hooting like a bugle,' I said to myself. Lali had gotten him to give up wearing his cap and let his hair grow; Pakistan had made him abandon his outfit of coarse, homespun cotton; and he had probably switched to wearing trousers of his own accord. His facial features were as unsightly as ever. Inattention had made his false teeth look uglier than the real teeth of someone who neglects taking care of them. His beady, lustreless eyes still darted as furtively as they had in the past, giving one the impression that he was fast and foxy, which in reality he was not. Perhaps because of the effects of ageing, ashy patches had appeared here and there on his face. His skin, which had never had any glow to begin with, now appeared as hard as buffalo hide.

After coming to Pakistan, Ehsan moved in with Mahmood, whose bungalow was located in the cantonment, and he never left there. A couple of times I rented a bicycle and went to see him, but he refused to go out with me anywhere. He asked how he could now face the same people before whom he had always denounced the creation of Pakistan, when he had been forced to take refuge there.

Farman would leave the bungalow early in the morning for town and return late at night. After ten days of sustained effort, he finally succeeded in having a house allotted to him in Krishan Nagar and a shop on Brandreth Road (where there used to be, and still is, a market for ironwork goods and machinery). Since Farman had worked in factories before, he knew a little about the iron and machinery business. Today he's a successful businessman and a factory owner worth several millions. In those early days, when refugees from India had not yet started to arrive in large numbers, an allotment, which took no more than a couple of days for other claimants, still took Farman a good ten days. And this was because the other claimants from his former city complained, 'He's a Congressite. So was his father who died in jail. Tell him to go back to India. What's he doing here anyway? This property is our right.' This would intimidate the junior employees of the claims office into prolonging action on Farman's request. But finally, a superior officer had the courage to recommend favourable action, arguing that now that Farman and his family were already here, they could be expected to live here permanently. No matter how one regarded them, they qualified as refugees, and hence deserved to be allotted a house to live in and a shop to earn their living from. To Farman's complainers the officer said, 'Forget about the past. Those who have come here are Pakistanis and have the same rights as other Pakistanis.'

My father too got it into his head to start a business. He managed to get a store filled with cloth allotted to himself. He named the store Zaheer & Son and started selling silk and satin. I said to Ehsan, 'Brother, why don't you take advantage of the wealth left behind by the Hindus? Make some effort and ask for a store or something.'

He said, 'I worked in a job back there and I'll do the same here. I won't breathe a word to anyone about my political views. That way I'll at least spare myself ridicule and embarrassment. And besides, I don't have any political views any more. Pakistan has come into being. May it last long. But it won't solve the problems for which we wanted to have the Partition in the first place.' The day Farman moved with Aapa into his allotted house in Krishan Nagar, Ehsan set out for Karachi where he found himself a job as a clerk in the accounts department of a British export–import company, eventually rising to the rank of superintendent. His superiors were happy with his diligence and his honesty, and his colleagues respected him for his courtesy and pleasing manners. To pay for his medical treatment, he borrowed the maximum allowable against his provident fund; his company contributed the balance as a gift.

The minute he saw me he yelled, laughing, 'Hey, here comes my buddy!' For a few moments he stood with his hands outstretched and his face beaming with affection, then he came forward and hugged me. Four of his friends, two men and two women, were with him. When they saw their guru welcoming a stranger so warmly, they stood up too. Ehsan had now developed a small potbelly which seemed unnatural on his otherwise slim frame, and his soiled, faded T-shirt looked tight around the middle. He seated me on the sofa next to him and then spoke to a girl, 'Tim, make some tea for him, and quickly please. Good girl.' Then he asked me to get up, saying, 'Let's go to the other room.

They'll be able to talk freely here and we'll be at ease there.'

For a long while we talked about his trip and surgery. He said, 'I had a strange experience. Two nights and one day just disappeared from my life as though they never existed and neither did I. It was like seeing a snippet, a brief glimpse of death. It gave me a taste of what death would be like. A total nothingness, where there is neither light nor darkness, neither sound nor silence, neither pain nor joy, nor sensation or consciousness. Just empty space. It's difficult to imagine absolute nothingness while one is still living. Sleep is different. We're alive during sleep, and actually, in a sense, more fully alive than when we're awake. The third day the doctor got me out of bed and made me walk without support. And I walked.'

In the meantime the girl came in and placed tea before us. She was about to leave when Ehsan asked, 'Did you offer tea to the other guests also?'

'Yes. They're already having theirs.' She lingered briefly, staring at Ehsan, just in case he might want her to do something else. When he didn't speak, she left. I asked, 'Yaar, what kind of name is this—Tim?'

'Such girls don't really have any names. Their parents give them one name, they call themselves by some other, and they give their clients yet another. I believe they do this to lose all sense of their identity, and they do it so totally that if they ever wanted to retrieve their identity, they wouldn't be able to. Perhaps this ruse allows them to assume and to derive false satisfaction from the assumption that while Tim is out walking the streets luring clients, the virginal Ruqaiya is still at home, as pure as ever.' He paused, thought for a while and then said, 'Perhaps it isn't really an assumption. It is the reality. After all, it's the body that's involved in those transactions, in order to support itself, never the heart. Anyway, as I was saying, every client calls them by the name of his choice. And I don't need to tell you that there's a name stuck in everyone's cranium which he carries with him to the grave.' As soon as he uttered those words, a loud bell sounded in my mind echoing Parveen's name. I had goosebumps all over. At first I flinched but then suddenly became sad. Ehsan was saying, 'This profession is really about filling the spaces left in men's hearts by other women. In other words, you could say these women are obliged to play the roles of men's former lovers. Which is all well and good. But the minute somebody begins to like them for themselves, their identity and individuality return. That's when they become the victims of crimes of passion. Even they don't know when someone has stopped using them to fill an empty space and started to love them for themselves. Now where there's love, there's bound to be jealousy. And where there's jealousy, there's also murder.'

Apparently Ehsan's flat had been open for such girls right from the beginning. They could come in any time, eat whatever was there or cook for themselves if they wanted to, wash and clean themselves there, even stay for two or three days if they needed a place, and leave any time they wanted to; no one stopped them. Ehsan had this yen for being in the company of females and talking to them. Numberless girls must have visited there, but the amazing thing was that he never formed any kind of liaison with any of them. They could not bring their clients to the flat, nor were they allowed to make deals with friends who visited him. But, of course, they were free to do as they wished outside the flat.

Ehsan said that it felt nice to have pretty girls in colourful clothes walking about the house. He didn't smoke in the past or even now, but his fascination with colours had taken him near and far in search of empty cigarette packets in his youth. He said, 'These girls are like empty cigarette packs. People use them and throw them away. Back in the old days I had to go looking for empty cigarette packs. But these days, they come here on their own. I give them a feeling of belonging, which they seldom get anywhere else in the world. They spend some time here which helps them to recuperate psychologically, as it were, and then move on. This girl, when she started coming here, gave her name as "Nilofar". I gave her the name "Tim"—because her eyes twinkled, like an oil-lamp. For some time she was called "Twinky", but then she became "Tim". When she's with the rest of us, she laughs, titters, chuckles and banters with the other girls. Then her face glows. But if she retreats into herself, that glow fades. It may even die out completely. When she recovers and joins in with the others again, the glow returns. When I take her aside and ask her what's the matter, she tells me her mother had a seizure again that morning. There wasn't a paisa in the house. She had to leave her mother unattended to go out and make some money to pay for her treatment. But that afternoon she still hadn't found a client; she'll try again in the evening. She worries that her mother will have another fit in her absence, or that she might already be dead when she gets home with the money. You're fond of writing stories, aren't you? Each of these girls is a complete novel in herself. I could give you enough material for ten or fifteen stories in one evening. These streetwalkers are really the most oppressed of their profession. Though everyone, of course, knows the truth about them, they're forced to keep up a façade of respectability in their own neighbourhoods and among their own relatives. The girls who sell themselves openly in the bazaar, on the other hand, have their whole "family-at-large" behind them. If the family is well off, they train their girls in singing and dancing. Then there's also the fact that this sort of profession isn't looked down on among their peers. Compared to these streetwalkers, even the girls of Lali's gypsy tribe have it better: at least their lives are psychologically more secure, because among them selling one's body isn't considered all that immoral. These street girls, on the other hand, are unskilled labourers with their bodies. And in the end, they're as good as dead as soon as their bodies begin to sag.'

I believe it was the memory of Lali that had driven Ehsan to turn his house into something of a shelter. Perhaps the idea that some day even Lali might come by, needing a respite from her arduous life, may also have been lurking somewhere in his mind. Lali had given him love and confidence, and had introduced him to sexuality. Her love was still alive in his heart. He never cared for the rich and powerful—their pretentiousness, as he would say, disgusted him—and he never aspired to become one himself. Some opportunities to engage in business did come his way, but he found his humble job far too satisfying to give up. In the same way, he despised women who were heavily made up or were vain about their beauty. His heart only went out to those who were like him, simple and oppressed by circumstances.

He remained an ascetic for a long time. There used to be a telephone operator in his office, a girl named Nazo. Her husband had run way to the States, leaving her and their two small children behind. Nazo's mother, who was paralysed, lived in Lahore, and Nazo had to send her money every month. The older child, a girl, went to some English elementary school. The younger child was a boy. Nazo had her own house but her salary was too meagre to meet all the expenses, so Ehsan brought her, along with the children, to his house. That way she at least was rid of her immediate financial problems. Nazo reasoned that so long as this fool remained sexually aloof, she ran the risk of being driven out of his house at any time. She trapped him, assuring him of her love, and it was decided that they would marry. Her first marriage was still intact, so she had to file for divorce. They ran around the courts for two, two and a half years. When at last the divorce came through, she ran away with some fat cat, leaving the children with Ehsan. He looked after them like his own. He would take the daughter to school every day on his motorcycle, lugging the son along as well. Two months later Nazo returned, full of airs, and whisked the children away with her in a car. Ehsan wept after they had left, and he grieved for a long time over having been misunderstood. He would have done all this anyway, even if that stupid woman hadn't deceived him in love. But it's impossible for someone dishonest to consider anybody honest. Ehsan's friends often brought liquor and consumed it at his place. He had no objection. After the children were wrenched away from him, he started drinking, at somebody's suggestion, to drown his sorrow. But it didn't sit well with him. It gave him a feeling of claustrophobia, accompanied by a loss of control over his limbs. He was anxious to snap out of this state, but intoxication takes its own time to wear off. He was afraid that the feeling of suffocation might become permanent.

Ehsan was so repentant about propagating the Congress ideology before Partition that he found it hard to support any other ideology afterwards. At a personal level, he was now influenced by socialism and regarded it as the only panacea for the poor and the downtrodden. But he never said a word to anybody in support of it, nor took any practical steps to promote it. He told me once: 'My friend, who knows, tomorrow even socialism may betray us, and to save my life a second time I might have to run for cover under the umbrella of capitalism. I'm a common man and I've learned the hard way that a common man had better not deviate from the ordinary political course, otherwise his wife and children will have to go through much suffering. While he has his belief in an idea or an ideology to sustain him through his misery, his poor family, who lack his conviction, are needlessly dragged along into much hardship by the complications created by him. There is no such thing as absolute truth in this world. Truth is always on the side of victory. Your father did the right thing, and Farman was also right in doing what he did after coming to Pakistan.'

In his adolescence and youth, the desire to gain India's freedom from British domination had reached the point of being a deep emotional crisis for Ehsan. But apart from nursing hatred and ill will for the British, he had done nothing practical to bring that freedom about. At most he'd hit his listeners with a fiery speech supporting the Congress during one of those political discussions that broke out in the side streets of our neighbourhood at the time, and then he'd walk away. Likewise, his second passion was the unity of the Islamic world and the upliftment of Muslims among the nations of the world. Whether the desire for Muslim unity was a consequence of his hatred for the British, or whether he had embraced the hatred of the British in the cause of Muslim unity was hard to tell. In any case, he never observed the trappings of religion. After coming to Pakistan, he adopted a somewhat Sufi-like attitude: 'Don't harm anyone; love everybody; serve everyone; each is right in his own way; the political maps and economic conditions of nations change automatically at their appointed time as ordained by nature; man's efforts to effect change are not likely to make any difference.' At one time he considered the Congress infallible; now, though, he conceded that 'Its leadership had become so entirely preoccupied with the mission to expel the British that they had lost touch with the realities of life around them. Trusting that the validity of this mission was an incontrovertible universal truth, its leadership had come to believe that once India was freed, all its citizens would live in peace and harmony for all time to come, and that all the country's problems and differences would be resolved forthwith. In their misguided assumption they completely failed to notice, much less do anything about, the lack of faith, the mistrust and the fear that was increasing continuously at the national level among a minority as visible as the Muslims. When they did finally direct their attention to the problem, it was too late. In their slowness, or rather, their delinquency, they stupidly assumed that the support of a few Muslim ulema was representative of the wishes of a hundred million Muslims. The general Indian temperament was, and still is, one of religious fanaticism. Despite having lived next to each other for a thousand years, the followers of every religion in this country are so intolerant of the followers of the others that they haven't made the slightest effort to understand them.'

He went on to say, 'Let me tell you what happened once. One time, which turned out to be the last time, Aapa and I went to visit my father in Lahore Central Jail. There the officials scheduled our visit for the next day. We had to spend the night in Lahore. Now, I don't remember how we got to the house where we spent the night. All I remember is that when I woke up the next morning and found myself in an unfamiliar place, I got terribly confused and agitated. It was an open rooftop with a single cot. I was lying on it and my mother was squatting on it nearby, the way she squatted on a railway platform waiting for the train, quiet and absent-minded. The gentle morning breeze felt pleasant. Once in a while the call of a milk-seller wafted in on the breeze and then vanished. Pots and pans began clanging, handpumps began moving. The melodious sounds of bhajan-chanting, accompanied by a harmonium, poured into my ears for the first time ever. I liked it. I got off the cot and moved around to take a look. Everywhere I glanced there was a sprawl of red-brick walls. I peered down into the courtyard. A long line of cots, with an assortment of bedding, appeared before me. Some people were still sound asleep. Others, limbering up, were walking about slowly, half-awake, taking care of their various needs. An elderly man was sitting in lotus position, as erect as if he were a statue. Astonished, I asked my mother what the man was doing. She said he was performing his morning *sandhya*. I asked what that was. She said it was their namaz. I said, then why didn't they say their namaz properly, as we did. My mother told me to shut up and stop talking nonsense.'

Ehsan looked towards me and resumed, 'Yaar, the Lahore

of those days was so amazing! So beautiful! The Mall, and the area east of it, which was settled after the arrival of the English! It looked as though somebody had built a tasteful assortment of large dazzling buildings, in a variety of attractive architectural styles, on the empty spaces in a park. Yellow-painted tongas on wide-open roads, their drivers wearing similar uniforms with a gleaming number engraved in brass on their turbans. In one such tonga, sitting on the back seat with Aapa, I started out, from God knows what neighbourhood, to see my father at the jail. The young son of the people we had stayed with the night before sat on the front seat next to the driver. Up until then, Aapa and I had travelled alone to the jails in far-off places in the Punjab, but here, at the insistence of our hosts, Aapa let the boy come along. He was to stay with us until he had seen us off at the station after the visit. When the tonga reached the Mall, my eyes fell on a cannon. I became curious and asked the boy about it. He told me it was the Sweepers' Cannon. It seemed like a strange object, with an even stranger name. I wondered in amazement why the sweepers would want to build such a thing and how. The cannon was mounted on a platform smack in the middle of the road. Surely, I thought, it must have meant something special to the English for them to display it so prominently. It was jet-black with rings of brass, enormous wooden wheels and a long, high neck. When we passed near it, I poked my head out through the canvas of the roof and the mudguard, and asked, "What does it do?" The boy said, "It gets stuffed with gunpowder and is fired at the enemy during a war." I asked, "Do the British use it to kill Indians?" The boy just smiled and kept quiet.

'I wasn't happy sitting in the back seat even before, but

now that so many new and interesting things were passing me by unobserved, it became essential to move to the front seat. Even though Aapa said I was being too restless and would fall off, I climbed into the front seat, partly with the boy's help and partly holding on to Aapa's shoulders. Woolner's life-size statue, in the posture of some great administrator with books in hand, stood on the side of the Mall in front of the Senate Hall gate. Across from it, in front of the gates of the museum, was the white marble statue of Sir Ganga Ram, sitting comfortably in a chair. Lajpat Rai's black statue—in which he is shown making a speech with his index finger raised—was also there somewhere. There were tall green trees, and behind them, even taller red-brick buildings. And there were flowers and shrubs in empty spaces here and there. No smell of fumes hung in the air, as it does nowadays. I was trying to drink everything in, wide-eyed and wonderstruck. The statues were a novelty for me; they seemed to add an elegance to the beauty of the Mall. When we passed in front of the Tollinton Market, there were no chicken feathers flying about nor was there any stench of rotting meat. The number of tongas, the volume of traffic, the activity and movement of people multiplied as our tonga moved forward. But there was no noise. Sweepers had been stationed at many places, with buckets and shovels, to remove the horse dung. At the centre of the General Post Office intersection, lush green grass glistened within a circular patch, with traffic flowing around it in an orderly fashion. There were giggling girls with the borders of their headgear flying about in the air, lively young schoolboys holding on to their books, office clerks, and at times, milky-white, golden-haired English ladies flying about on their bicycles. Now and then a shiny car would whiz by between two rows of tongas. It was a time when the exhaust from automobiles and motor-rickshaws hadn't yet sullied the pristine sunshine, made ever so agreeable by gusts of the fresh morning breeze. The dense foliage of jamun and peepal shaded both sides of the road. The Ganga Ram Trust Building and the horseshoe-shaped Dayal Singh Trust Building stood in the sun smiling, radiant, clean, their plasters intact. It was the same with the Lakshmi Building in Regal Square and the Dinga Singh Building in the Beadon Road Square. The official buildings, of course, were imposing and majestic, but these privately built structures also had an impressive beauty and grace, a character all their own, which didn't fail to affect the onlooker. They all played a major role in making the Mall a part of the landscape of your dreams. In those days these buildings were still young, not decrepit and rundown as they are today. The marble statue of Queen Victoria sitting on a throne was ruling India from under a *barahdari* at Charing Cross. Behind it was the grand Assembly Hall, with the Shah Din Building in front of it on one side and the Freemasons' Hall on the other, all adding to the splendour of the Mall.

'I turned around to look at my mother. She was gazing God knows where, wrapped in her chador, lost in her thoughts, unaffected by all these wondrous sights which were stirring up so much commotion in me. I was completely enraptured by the magical charm of this city. I said to her, "Why don't you leave me here? I'll walk about the streets during the day and go sleep with Father in the jail at night." Aapa remained silent.

'We met Father in some officer's room. All I can remember

is that a small, lean, bespectacled man came and sat in a chair. Aapa was crying, while the man did most of the talking. I didn't feel at all eager to meet this stranger, nor did I know how to meet, if necessary, someone called "Father". So I occupied myself by scrutinizing the room and its furnishings. When the allotted time was up, the man who was "Father" patted me on the head and said, "Put your heart into your studies, do you hear?" I nodded in acknowledgement. I was in a big hurry to get out of there and start our tonga ride through the streets all over again. As Aapa stepped out of the jail's vestibule, she suddenly began crying so bitterly that I was stunned at first. Then I started to cry myself. The boy who was waiting for us outside made us sit down in the shade of a peepal in the yard which faced the entrance. He brought her some water. After about half an hour, Aapa was finally able to pull herself together enough to walk to the road and get inside the tonga. Today, fifty years later, I feel that India was bound to get her freedom one way or another, if not in 1947, then maybe in 1957. Father gave up his life and squandered his property for no reason at all. He yielded us up as well, especially Aapa, to a suffering whose deep scars still persist today.'

For a long while Ehsan and I sat in silence, each lost in his own thoughts. Meanwhile Tim came in. She turned on the light and then asked, 'Why are you two sitting in the dark? Supper is ready.'

Ehsan asked, 'Have Siddiqi sahib and Manzoor sahib eaten?'

'They waited for you playing chess for quite a while. Half an hour ago they left. Chandni's gone too. And I'm leaving now.'

'Listen, have you eaten?'

'I'm not hungry.'

'Nonsense. Go bring the food here. We'll all eat together. And then we'll pray for you.'

She chuckled and went away to bring the food. Ehsan asked me, 'Yaar, would you have fifty rupees with you?' I took out a fifty-rupee note and gave it to him. When Tim came in with the food, he gave the money to her saying, 'Take it. Buy medicines for your mother. The money is not mine, it's Saeed sahib's. So you aren't required to pay it back either.'

She clutched the note quietly in her fist. She wanted to thank me but felt too overwhelmed to open her mouth. An uneasy smile flashed across her face and then faded. After the meal, she grabbed her purse and left. Because we had been busy with eating, and the conversation had taken a different turn, the sadness that had descended upon our hearts lifted.

I said, 'Ehsan, did the Congress not value your father's life enough to offer your family protection during the riots?'

'No, it wasn't like that. They did offer to protect us. But whether they did anything for their Muslim workers at the national level, I don't know. While we were still in our old house near the railway tracks, we received a message saying that they would send us to some safe place if we wanted. Then later, after we moved to Sharifpura, Pandit Krishan Lal, the city president of the Congress, came himself in a tonga looking for us. It was on the same day that you arrived to take us along with Mahmood, but it was a couple of hours earlier. We just about fainted seeing him at our doorstep. Farman said, "For heaven's sake, what's this? Coming to a Muslim area all alone?"

'Pandit-ji said, "Don't worry about me. No one will harm

me. I'm here in one piece, am I not? So what's the worry?" He seated Farman, Aapa and me in front of him and said, "You know the situation here. It's dangerous for you to stay in this city any longer. Of that I'm sure. I suggest that you move to Delhi. Arrangements have already been made for an army escort to protect you during the move and for you to have a place to stay after you get there. If you wish to remain in Delhi, you're welcome. As a matter of fact, the whole of UP is perfectly peaceful. But if you want to go to Lucknow instead, that can be arranged. In two or three months, when conditions have returned to normal, you can come back. Riots can't go on forever. This madness has to end one day."

'Aapa replied, "How can we live apart from our loved ones? Just think, my daughter and son-in-law are in Lahore. They have to live there. How can I abandon them? All of our relatives are waiting to move to Pakistan. It is they who give our lives a measure of happiness and well-being. How can we possibly live alone in India without them? You took so much trouble. We shall never forget your kindness for as long as we live."

'He said, "This is no favour, sister. It's my duty. Brother Bashir Ahmad made the freedom of India possible by sacrificing his life. His children and you will make both India and us proud by deciding to live here. I beg you, don't leave. All this uproar will die down in a few days. Soon everything will be all right." Aapa said, "For better or for worse, we've made up our minds to leave with our family. If conditions get better, we'll come back."'

Then Ehsan looked at me and said, 'Yaar, I think Aapa made a wise decision. In a population of hundreds of thousands, how many people does it take to make up a man's world? A few friends, some relatives, a handful of acquaintances and enemies—the rest is all a jungle even if it's a city of a million people. Nature has designed man to live in a small world. How far can he see? A few miles across a sea or a desert, even less if he's in a city. How far can he walk? Twenty or twenty-five miles. That's all.'

'When Aapa declined the offer, did you say anything?'

'There was nothing to say; after all, she'd put the matter to rest so firmly. Though I did think it wouldn't have hurt to take a free ride to Lucknow or Delhi and see a bit of the world. But it would have been a pretty costly ride. We would never have made it here.'

Out of Sight

It was an August afternoon. The sun, lodged in a sky washed clean by the rain, stared continuously at the world with its wrathful eyes. By that time, the traffic had died down and the main bazaar of the town of Sultanpur had become completely deserted. The pitch-black road lying senseless in the middle of the bazaar, soaking wet with perspiration, had taken on an even darker hue. The shopkeepers sat quietly in their shops behind awnings fastened to bamboo poles extending out to the road. What wretch would leave his house in such weather to go shopping? Sitting on the chair inside his shop, Ismail saw his friend's eight- or ten-year-old son, Mubashshir, pass by under his awning, walking backwards with a satchel around his neck. A smile suddenly appeared on Ismail's face. Kids will be kids, he thought. Feeling bored and alone since he couldn't find anything to interest him, he had devised this private pastime of walking home backwards. Ismail called him over: 'Hey, Mubashshir, come here!'

'Coming, Baba-ji.' Saying that, the boy climbed the two wooden-plank stairs and stood facing Ismail. His demeanour showed respect and his wondering eyes were asking, 'What's the matter?'

'Why are you walking backwards? Want to bump into some bicyclist or pedestrian?'

'No, Baba-ji, I'm careful. Every now and then I turn around to look.'

'Don't act silly. Walk straight up the road, face forward. Do you understand?' The boy said yes, and as he started going down the two steps, Ismail asked, 'Is your father back from Lahore yet?'

'No. He'll be back by this evening.'

When the country was partitioned, Ismail was hiding in Amritsar, a major city in East Punjab, where he had arrived two weeks before, having fled his ancestral town of Gobindpur looking for a place of refuge. From Amritsar, he set out for Lahore with the horde of other migrants. For six months he languished in a cramped refugee camp, chock-full of people like himself. An old acquaintance at the camp told him that the Muslims of Gobindpur, at least those who had survived, had all gone to Sultanpur. Ismail went there looking for them. The majority of Gobindpur Muslims had been massacred by the Sikhs, burned alive inside their own houses. How could he have found them? One person from his own family, whose ancestors had belonged to Gobindpur, had indeed arrived in Sultanpur, but he had gone with his family to Delhi and settled there about ten months before the Partition. Later, he came straight to Pakistan from Delhi. He wouldn't have known what had transpired in Gobindpur after Ismail's escape: how and in what form the final catastrophe had arrived, how Gobindpur's inhabitants were killed, or who the killers were. Were they from the town itself or from outside? And if anyone had survived, where could they be?

In Sultanpur Ismail ran into an old college friend who was stationed there as a government official. He helped Ismail get a tiny store, which was a bangles-and-make-up shop, and the allotment to an equally small house in a neighbourhood a short distance away. Those were the only properties left by that time. The official workers broke the seal of the shop and found everything inside covered in dust. On the facing wall there was a picture with Guru Nanak Dev in the middle sitting in a contemplative posture. Bhai Bala sat a little behind, cooling him with a peacock-feather fan. On the other side of the picture Bhai Mardana could be seen with a rubab in his hands. Ismail felt as if the rubab would begin playing on its own and Guru Nanak Dev would intone:

> Onkaar sat-naam karta purkh, nirbhau, nirvair, Akaal Murat Ajuni seh bhang gur parsaad . . .[1]

But the Guru did not ask for the rubab to be played, nor did he say anything himself. Perhaps he was upset that a Sikh's shop was being given over to a Muslim. But then, Ismail reasoned: Why would the Guru think such thoughts? To him all human beings were equal. Such musings were the province of the worldly, not of the Sufis and dervishes. Ismail had sung the Guru's song about the Unity of the Godhead from grades five to ten during his student days at the Khalsa High School in Gobindpur and had often wondered what part of it went against the preaching of Islam. Why don't the Sikhs and Muslims feel affectionate towards each other? Only much later did he realize that the issue was not about a difference in religious beliefs, but about the arbitrary manner in which the majority group acted. Considering the minority group low

[1] There is but one God, True is his name; Author of this World; Immortal His form; without fear, without enmity; unborn, self-illumined; Perceived only through the Guru's grace.

and powerless, they never tired of belittling or humiliating it.

Being the owner of a bangles-cum-make-up shop meant procuring numberless little items and selling them largely to women and children. He didn't like this arduous, piecemeal work. A few days later he put all his merchandise up for sale, even at a loss, and opened a drugstore in the same location. While changing the character of the store so radically he often wondered if its original owner would have done the same. Perhaps not. Perhaps he himself shouldn't have done it either. How unhappy the original owner would have been to find out what had been done to his shop.

From a full-grown young man, Ismail had now turned old and grizzly, but he'd been running the same tiny drugstore with the contentment of a bhikshu, a religious mendicant. He'd established a tenor of total contentment between himself and the world, with no desire at all to either become affluent or raise his standard of living. Without any expectations from life, he was blithely enjoying a freedom from all cares. A single man does not have many wants, and the shop was taking care of his needs sufficiently. That didn't mean he had always had such a Sufic point of view about life. Like every young man, his heart too was once filled with longings and desires. But what he had observed during his six-month stay at the refugee camp brought him gradually, slipping and sliding, even without receiving a lesson in Sufism from anyone, to this point of view. He had noticed at the camp how the pressure of personal wants drove men to change their attitudes constantly and adopt new ones; how people trapped between personal needs and selflessness, between animal instincts and human obligations, constantly bobbed up and down as if caught in a whirlpool. He witnessed hundreds of stories taking shape before him, most ending in victory for selfishness and success for unprincipled conduct. Sometimes the winner's face, acknowledging his own meanness and vulgarity, oozed regret at first, but as time passed he was devoid of this constraint as well. The veneer of morality, justice, scruples, charity, good manners soon fell away, revealing the green tarnished copper of selfishness underneath. Disgrace became an everyday phenomenon, and nobody died from the pain. Tight-lipped, they all bore it as if it were a providential command.

There were only two classes of people at the camp: one despairing of money, without any hope for the future, a crowd of shivering, thirsting, humiliated people; and the other a smaller, happier group of ecstatic tyrants. Ismail made up his mind then and there that if there ever was an occasion for him to migrate again, he would rather die with his kith and kin in Gobindpur than go elsewhere looking for safety.

He had been married once, but his wife passed away. They had a child, but he too died a few months after the mother. Later on, Ismail never thought about marriage. He only had one passion—reading the newspapers. The discordance and sweetness in familial relationships, the tremulous tension caused by myriad anxieties over wives and children, the indecisions and worries about profit and loss—life's many facets, each with its own taste and flavour. He had to, and did, obtain all those tastes, enjoyments, sensations and tremors through his newspapers as he walked along the tracks of life maintaining his poise and balance. He bought one newspaper himself; two or three he borrowed from others. To look at English newspapers, he went to the Committee Reading Room. He was a patriotic Pakistani and a believing Muslim, even though he'd never offered a prayer nor observed any of the other rites of his religion. Once a year, on Eid-ul-Fitr, he would visit the mosque; if he missed that occasion, the whole matter would be deferred to next year.

At sunset, after the customers from the villages had returned home, the bazaar became deserted. At that time, two or three shopkeepers the same age as Ismail would come and sit with him to exchange views on current events and conditions. He would entertain them with tea and sweet beverages, and based on his own perusal of the newspapers, would express his views with great enthusiasm on political, social, economic, national and international issues. At times, bitter arguments and differences of opinion would break out. If the tempers started to become frayed, he suddenly clammed up, which invariably caused the other person's steam to evaporate quickly. A certain tension and displeasure would grip the group, and gradually, both the partisan and the impartial discussants would get up and take their leave. Within twenty-four hours, however, both parties would forget their earlier acrimony and join again and conversation would begin to flow on one topic or another. Occasionally, Bashir Ahmad also joined this company for gossip.

Bashir Ahmad was the youngest of them all. When Ismail, alone, and Bashir, with his family and relations, reached Pakistan as refugees from various parts of eastern Punjab, Ismail was in the last year of his BA and Bashir was just a toddler crawling on his knees. Ismail became friends with Bashir's father, Chaudhry ʿAta Muhammad, and their friendship endured until the latter died. He was a very sincere, loving and compassionate man; but one of his habits irked Ismail immensely. During his life Ismail had come across many Ahmadis—even here in Sultanpur, at least a couple dozen of them had been buying medicines from him. But the manner in which ʿAta Muhammad adhered to Ahmadism wasn't visible in anyone else. No matter what the topic of conversation, or how unrelated it was to anything remotely religious, ʿAta Muhammad would blurt out what the Promised Messiah had said about it, quote from the sayings of Mirza Ghulam Ahmad, and attempt to twist the topic to fit the saying. An even more difficult stage arrived when he would recite, in a sing-song voice, the religious verses of notable Ahmadi elders in support of his arguments and, because of his lamentable lack of taste, would recite them without regard for the demands of metre and rhyme. Not without a pinch of the salt of firm belief could one swallow this recitation, and no one in the assembly had this salt available to him—no one, that is, except ʿAta Muhammad.

Neither Ismail nor any of his friends had any trouble with ʿAta Muhammad's belief, nor any objection to his emotional attachment to Mirza sahib and his family. They all firmly believed that everyone had the right to their own faith and to accept whomsoever they wanted as their idol. This was an acknowledged fact like a universal truth which no one ever even questioned. Once, when ʿAta Muhammad wasn't present, Shaikh Sardar Ali, the cloth merchant, quietly objected that Islam had been a perfect religion, complete in every aspect, so why did the Ahmadis need to introduce a new prophet? This wasn't something the Sardar could have uttered in Chaudhry sahib's presence, deferring to civility and the latter's age. And even if he had tried, one of the group, or perhaps Ismail himself, would have forbidden him from turning the get-together into an arena for religious discord.

In any case, no one gave any importance to Shaikh Sardar Ali's comment, for it would have dragged on endlessly and, besides, he himself didn't insist on pursuing it—although, in 1953, an anti-Ahmadi movement had already sprung up that resulted in much bloodshed and many incidents of arson. The rioters assassinated a goodly number of Ahmadis and torched the estates of several of them. Numberless Ahmadis had to abandon their homes and go into hiding. The police and the army also gunned down many rioters. In order to restore peace and order, the Pakistani government imposed martial law within the city limits of Lahore. The situation became so depraved that it seemed as though the days of 1947 had turned around and come back. When the tumult subsided, people forgot the entire sordid episode as if nothing so life-wrenching had ever happened.

When a stone is thrown into a stagnant pool and splits open the scum on the surface, you think the surface will never be whole again, but it soon comes together as if it had never split in the first place. One major factor that made the creation of Pakistan possible was the establishment of religious tolerance among the various factions of the Muslim population. Muhammad Ali Jinnah was a follower of the Shiʿa denomination, yet every faction submitted to his orders and instructions without the least hesitation, and acknowledged him as their Quaid-e-Azam, their great leader. The spirit of religious harmony created in those early days seemed to have been shattered permanently in 1953, but as soon as the agitators of the disturbances, who were after political gains, were put behind bars, one had the impression that the nation's previous harmony had been restored without suffering any impairment.

The Munir Inquiry Commission dragged on for months. The common man wasn't particularly interested in it, but the fear in the faces and eyes of the Ahmadis was only too visible even days after the establishment of peace and order. They were scarred badly. Their trust in their fellow citizens in the affairs of daily life was shaken, their sense of pride was wounded, as though a dear friend had slapped you across the face. Their social life was restricted to their co-religionists. It took them years to recover from their state of uncertainty. The Munir Inquiry report gave them some hope. Following the riots, Chaudhry ʿAta Muhammad became taciturn for some time, and his attendance at the gatherings at Ismail's shop was considerably less frequent. It took him about two years to finally return, though slowly, to his former mood. Although the fright and terror of the days of rioting were soon obliterated from the minds of the common folk, a few of the jokes that sprang up then are still being repeated for some belated enjoyment.

Ismail loved all of his friends, but the sincere attachment he felt for Bashir wasn't shared by anyone else. Of course, there were reasons for his attachment. First off, Bashir had grown up right in front of his eyes. If his own son had lived, he would have been roughly the same age as Bashir. Secondly, Bashir was easily achieving everything in life that Ismail had once hoped for himself, and misfortune hadn't so far thought of waylaying him. If someone close achieves what had been your own burning ambition in life, treating that achievement as your own and sharing in it isn't just a sign of magnanimity; it's also a rare natural gift that consoles the person deprived of that achievement. He may still have deep regret all through his life, but at least he doesn't cry any more.

When Bashir did his matriculation from Sultanpur and entered intermediate-level classes in Lahore, Ismail felt as though he was living his own past vicariously, as if time had turned around softly and carried him back to the days when he himself had passed his matriculation from Gobindpur and joined the college at Amritsar. In time, Bashir completed his BA, which Ismail had had to abandon because of Partition. While still in Gobindpur, he read about the communal riots in newspapers, but he never imagined they would turn out to be so bloody. That all his relatives—some one hundred and fifty people—would be slaughtered down to the last man, was indeed something hard to imagine! His parents, brothers, sisters, and all his close relatives had been massacred by the Sikhs. By contrast, Bashir, his parents, his kith and kin had all arrived safely in Sultanpur without encountering any bloodshed or devastation. They didn't have to suffer any mental or physical jolts, whereas Partition had turned Ismail's whole life upside down. What, then, was the point in lamenting the failure to complete his BA degree. If all his plans had steadily materialized as he had hoped, he could have built his life's edifice systematically brick by brick. Now it was just a tomb of regrets lodged deep in his heart. When Bashir finished his law degree, Ismail was overjoyed. It was as if he had himself become a lawyer and, come next morning, would don his black coat and go to the courts in Gobindpur, while his father, putting on a coat of mock humility but actually full of pride, would go around introducing him to the other lawyers. None of this was destined to happen. Rather than Ismail practising law in Gobindpur, it was Bashir who would practise it in Sultanpur. Just as Bashir and his entire community of some twenty families had settled on both sides of a street in a Sultanpur neighbourhood, so Ismail longed to have settled down with his community the same way. But how could that be? His folks were never allowed to reach Pakistan, dispatched as they were to the next world before they could ever set foot in their new homeland.

Bashir's street was closed at the farther end; the area beyond was occupied by cultivated fields. The homes, most of them already built above or below each other, were joined by interconnecting doors. The Hindus and Sikhs who lived on this street before were likely related to one another; that must have been why they had arranged for this convenience. Houses without this convenience were now fitted with new doors and, if you entered the first house, you could now easily reach the last house without having to step out into the street.

As soon as Mubashshir came into the house, he called out: 'Amma, I want water.'

'Want me to bring you lassi?'

'Yes.'

'All right, then go to the bazaar and fetch fifty paise worth of ice. You wouldn't want to drink warm lassi, would you? If you get ice, even I might have a glass.'

'I can't go now. Borrow some ice from Phupha's house.'

'Is this any time to knock at the connecting door? Who knows, they might be eating or resting! I don't want to bother them over a trifle. Besides, your Phupha doesn't like people knocking at his door whenever the fancy strikes them.'

'I don't want to go out now. I'll drink it warm. Just bring it to me.'

'Come on, son, don't be stubborn. The ice-seller is just down the street. You'll be back in a second. You could have already brought it home by now. Here, take this piece of cloth and the eight-anna piece. Come on, hurry up.'

After gulping down the glass of cold lassi, Mubashshir said, 'Amma, starting tomorrow I'm not going to school.'

'Why? Why not?'

'The boys use swear words.'

'Look who's talking! You're just as foul-mouthed! The amount of rubbish you boys spill out while playing in the street—don't I hear it? You must be using their language back at them. Of course it'll provoke them, and they'll get riled up.'

'No, Amma, you don't understand. There are three or four boys who make fun of Hazrat Sahib and Ahmadiyyat. The other boys start grinning and laughing. They don't curse me, they swear at the abusers. Who should I curse in return?'

The befuddled mother became quiet. She had no idea what response she could possibly give to her child. Silence often becomes the shield of a weak person. She thought about the matter for a bit and then decided to persuade the boy that in a situation such as this it was best to keep quiet.

'Try not to curse them. Let them swear as much as they want. You just stay put. Don't you have any friends in class?'

'Of course I do, but they don't open their mouths. Only when we're alone, then they tell me how rotten those boys are and that they shouldn't be saying what they do. But my friends don't dare face those boys in my presence.'

'You should have talked to your teacher.'

'I did.'

'What happened then?'

'At first he laughed. After a while he said he would admonish those boys. But he hasn't done anything so far, not even called them over to talk to them.'

Sunk in despair and caught in the whirlpool of a similar foreboding, both mother and son were quietly wondering for a long time. Just as a drowning man grasps at a straw, the presence of one gave confidence to the other. At last, Mubashshir broke the silence and repeated his earlier resolve: 'Amma, I'm not going to school tomorrow. They'll swear at me again, and the boys will laugh again.'

Mothers quickly see through the troubles that ail their children. Nature perhaps has endowed them with this special ability. Mubashshir's mother had perhaps suffered a similar ordeal during her own schooldays and so could empathize with the boy's heartache and understand his helplessness at the debasement caused by his classmates—although in her own days it couldn't have gone beyond bitter verbal exchanges. She pulled Mubashshir towards her and wrapped him in her arms. Tears welled up in her eyes as she stroked his head. But she also knew that if she allowed those tears to fall from her eyes, Mubashshir would lose what little courage he had. She had to hold them back. And she did. But the effort gave her eyes the same dry, vacant look of people trapped in slavery.

'Son, how many places will you avoid going to? Have faith in God; He Himself will do justice by us. This is nothing. Prepare yourself for worse to come. If you give up hope now, how will you withstand the future? Tomorrow, your father will himself walk you to school and talk to the teacher. Have no dealings with those boys. Let them say what they will. They'll tire out on their own in a day or two and quiet down.'

*

When the British made up their minds to quit India, the news spread like a rumour to the most distant rural areas of the country dotted with villages and stricken by ignorance and poverty. People who should have jumped with joy, instead, suddenly became hushed, as if overwhelmed by some unexpected news of a mishap. Everybody seemed to be whispering fearfully: What was to happen now? And how? Mired in by this uncertainty, they were beset by a thousand different worries and anxieties of their own. They couldn't believe the land that had comforted and sustained them like a mother's lap, whose soil had for generations received the dust of their ancestors, was not only going to withdraw its support, but even spit them out like bitter fruit. And not just these people, even those who had lived and breathed politics every day of their lives couldn't believe that whole populations would be shunted off to another place merely on religious grounds—something unparalleled in human history.

In those days, Hindu–Muslim violence had spread like an epidemic in many places in India—today in Noakhali, tomorrow in Bihar, the day after in Naushehra. The temperament of the people had so changed that they became indifferent to the agonizing deaths of the innocents and to the helplessness of their descendants. What concerned them most was whether the followers of the other religion were killed in greater or smaller numbers. A sigh of relief if the number was great, and if not, worry over a plan for revenge. Humanity was being slaughtered, but Man had been left out of the count. The only countables were either Hindus, Sikhs or Muslims. As 6 June 1948, the date on which Britain had announced it would quit India—which some believed and others thought a lie—drew nearer, the sense of unease and fear increased. And in the larger cities, it was followed by frequent stabbing incidents. That was perhaps one way to verify the truthfulness of the announcement. Sometimes the situation in the country seemed to change rapidly, but at other times the country seemed to wallow in the same age-old inertia. In any case, a stifling fear of death was sinking its claws deeper and deeper into people's hearts in that uncertain atmosphere.

Because all the colleges had been closed down, Ismail, now in his final year before graduation in Amritsar, returned home to Gobindpur, travelling the eighty-three miles by bus and train. During that journey, he observed for the first time unmistakable flames of hatred and aversion for him in the eyes of his unknown Hindu and Sikh co-travellers, whereas before those eyes had exuded indifference. Hindus constituted the major part of the population in his ancestral town and owned just about every kind of business. Eight or ten lawyers and two or three doctors practised here. And the town of some forty thousand only had about seventy Muslim households, located some distance away in a small settlement at its outer edge. All the services, which were the responsibility of the area committee to provide, were practically non-existent in this settlement. By and large the Muslims belonged to the weaver or oil-pressing castes and were still plying their established ancestral trades. It's another matter that those castes, originally Hindu, had converted to Islam somewhere along the way, which didn't improve their social status or financial standing. The town's area was pretty wide and many far-flung villages were encompassed within it. The landholders were few; all of them

Sikhs who generally cultivated their own farms. If tenant cultivators were employed, they too tended to be Sikhs. There, population-wise, Sikhs predominated. The workers in the villages were Muslim, all low-caste kammis (service castes). The followers of Gugga Pir, the sweepers and leather-handlers, were in addition to the kammis and, as everywhere else, were considered creatures a notch below human. They had no particular social colour, or cultural shape or form. Very much like water, they adopted the habits and manners of whatever majority they found themselves amongst, even naming their children after those of the majority.

Although Guru Nanak had given mankind a manifest lesson in throwing caste distinctions overboard, it hadn't worked out quite that way in practice. A sweeper or leather-handler could convert to Sikhism and would then be branded a religious Sikh, but socially, he would still be treated as an untouchable. For those who touched or handled human waste, their own being remained a veritable term of abuse. They might do anything, live anywhere, but they always remained sweepers or leather-handlers. They were considered the lowest of the low because of the accident of their birth. The attitude of the Muslim society towards them and towards the new converts from among them was no different from that of the Hindus and Sikhs towards their own lowest castes.

Ismail's grandfather worked the oil press all through his life, and Ismail's father, after graduating from the eighth grade at Khalsa High School, decided to become a Hindu lawyer's scribe rather than ply his ancestral trade, wishing ardently for his son to receive an education and become a lawyer. And just when it seemed that dream might come true, he and his entire family were swallowed alive by the whirlpool of the communal riots. The news of bloody Hindu–Muslim riots came in from different parts of the country, hundreds of miles away, splattered across the front pages of the newspapers. Whenever Ismail saw such news, a tremor ran through his body and a wriggling fear began troubling his mind. But life, spread out in the streets around the Committee Reading Room, crawled drowsily along as usual like an ox tied to an oil press. Simple farmers and their equally unsophisticated women came from the villages to buy necessities and innocently haggled with the shrewd Hindu shopkeepers. Never before had the thought crossed Ismail's mind that he had been engulfed by a majority of non-Muslims. It was the newspapers that awakened this feeling in him. When he read in the day's papers that Master Tara Singh had unsheathed his sword on the steps of the Assembly Chambers in Lahore and declared as he waved it with a flourish, 'It is the power of the sword that will now decide the matter. The Sikhs are ready. We have to bring the Muslims to their senses,' the thought occurred to him that if someone in the reading room jumped up to kill him, he would not know how to defend himself, and could do nothing except die quietly. The thought of the lurking danger gave way to a fear of dying, which began to mushroom inside him like a nuclear cloud. Initially vague, the dread soon assumed a distinct shape. Like a stormy river, it rushed towards him hissing and screaming. He wanted to flee somewhere, but his feet, as often happens in dreams, refused to budge from the reading room floor.

Time and again Ismail wondered at the fact that no one had so far relayed Master Tara Singh's message to these people—a flock of sheep roaming around the bazaar, busily foraging for whatever they could find, a bush here, a lump of grass there. Even if they knew how to read the newspapers and did read them, nothing would stir them until someone angry and red-faced got on top of a high platform to make a determined effort to incite them and, in a divinely commanding voice, unleashed his fury proclaiming that the crafty scheming Muslims were the enemy of the Sikhs; that Muslims had made all kinds of plans to demolish their faith and destroy them; that Muslims were the enemy of the ten Gurus and reviled them; that now the Sikhs had exposed all their wicked schemes and there was no cure except to kill them all—only then would they pounce upon him like wild beasts. Ismail's fear of immediate danger did ultimately let up, and his wildly palpitating heart and heaving breath did calm down. Nonetheless, he came to realize that, given the situation in the country, it wouldn't be long before someone ferocious and red-faced arrived and ordered them to commence the genocide.

Although the fear of imminent death had been temporarily averted for him at the time, he could distinctly hear the danger ticking away like a time bomb for him, for his parents, his brothers and sisters and all the other Muslims of the town. Now, though, the majority, in spite of its potential to crush and trample, and quietly busy with its daily chores like a tamed wild animal, looked harmless and innocuous enough. Watching this same flock of sheep, no one could say that one day it would turn into a pack of vicious beasts. A person could not trust such a brute for long. At other times he felt that he had no reason to fear harm from the Sikh majority. After all, he had been living with them for ages in a state of mutual trust; if they hadn't hurt him so far, why would they do it now? His real fear came from 'the shadow', whose dreadful, furious, incendiary eyes followed his and every other Muslim's smallest move from behind every tree, door, wall and roof. The majority was just a tool—a lifeless tool with no will of its own; what made it work was the same devilish 'shadow'. He trembled with fear to think of the future.

He left the reading room and wearily returned to his house in a lane in one of the town's densely populated areas. His father had rented this house from a Hindu. At the entrance to the lane, bordering the main road, stood the lawyer Lala Ram Dayal's gargantuan three-storeyed house, one of whose doors opened on to Ismail's lane. Ismail's father worked as a scribe for this lawyer. After reaching home, a stupefied Ismail approached his mother who was sitting on a *peerhi*, sautéing some food in a cooking pot. He stood silently in front of her and wondered how best to broach the subject without scaring her, while still letting her appreciate the seriousness of the deteriorating situation. He was still wondering when his mother looked up and asked, 'What's happened, Ismail? Why are you looking so pale?'

'Mother, riots have broken out throughout the country; doesn't look as though they'll let up any time soon. Thousands have been killed. Gobindpur is filled with Sikhs and Hindus. We're in danger here. Mother, they're going to kill us and all the other Muslims in town and burn down our houses.'

'Come on! Why would they do that? We haven't done anything to them, have we? You talk as if the Hindus and Sikhs have just dropped in here out of nowhere today. Why, son, we've been living with them all along, ever since the world was created. Never had the slightest disagreement. You've become delusional. Is that what education does?'

Her serenity flustered him. 'Don't you know the whole country is on fire? There are riots everywhere. And here you want to know why they would kill us. Why were innocent Muslims killed in Noakhali? Why were Muslims mass murdered in Bihar? Only after they fall on you suddenly with swords drawn, then you'll know.'

'Go somewhere quiet and do your studies. Such things only take place in big cities. Nothing will happen here. Have faith. You don't want us to just get up and leave our house and home, do you? Just because of riots? And anyway, where do you want us to go? Has anything like this ever happened? Go, God will protect us.'

Just then someone knocked at the door. Ismail went out and saw that two of his old schoolmates, Sunder Singh and Brij Narayan Sahni, had come to see him. He opened the sitting room and asked them to have a seat. The room only had two chairs and a bed that was laid out. Sunder Singh picked up the books scattered on the bed and set them to one side, and then half stretched himself out on it. Sahni and Ismail took the chairs. Both guests felt as comfortable and informal as when they were in their own houses. After graduating from high school, Sunder Singh got himself a job as a clerk with the Municipal Committee, while Sahni, when he felt able to, helped his father in his small bangles-and-make-up store. However, Sahni spent most of his time reading communist literature or travelling from one village to another, forming farmers' organizations. After doing some reading on his own, Sunder Singh adopted the same line of thinking as Sahni. Their genuine feelings and their desire to do something truly worthwhile had, of course, not failed to affect Ismail. However, since he belonged to a socially and economically somewhat depressed minority, he felt his primary responsibility lay in extricating Gobindpur's Muslims from their backwardness, rather than worrying about the state of the whole of mankind. Another reason he couldn't join them in working for the party was that without a conception of God it was impossible for him to bring the universe and its operation into his focus of understanding. He was as much of a communist sympathizer and a Muslim in those days as he remained throughout his life.

'Hey, Sunder, how come you aren't in office today?' Ismail asked.

'Sunday, my dear fellow. And Sahni, as you know, is free almost every day. We hadn't seen you in quite a while, so we decided to inquire after you today.'

'Did you read Master Tara Singh's statement in the papers today?'

'Yeah, wouldn't you say he's boiled over a bit too much?'

Ismail said, 'But one gets the impression from the papers that the Sikhs approve of his declaration of war against Muslims.'

'Many of Master Tara Singh's close relatives were murdered in Pindi. Their houses were also burned down. Perhaps Master-ji is provoking the Sikh community to exact his own revenge. This isn't politics, but downright deceitfulness. In any case, they're not interested in real politics, only in playing with the feelings of gullible people, whom they do their best to warn that their religion is in great danger. And all this to blackmail their own community! The dazzling light of the twentieth century has completely blinded the common man who's been groping around in the darkness. Feeling helpless, he walks right into the bosom of religion, and his smooth-tongued leaders, after showing him sympathy, make him do whatever they want.'

Ismail said, 'Yeah, sure, that's how it is. And it will take ages to cure this ignorance. But what will happen to us in the meantime?'

'What do you mean?' Sunder asked.

'Amazing! You, so well informed and even you need to be told! Oh, well, you're right too, in your own way. Only the one who wears the shoes knows where they pinch. All the heat from the raging fire of the riots is for me, not you. The sword of death is dangling over my head, not yours. Okay, if you don't understand, let me make it plain for you: When are you "infidels" going to make short work of the few Muslims hemmed in by the enemy majority in a town as far-flung as Gobindpur?'

Both Sunder and Sahni cackled, and seeing them laugh, Ismail began to laugh too.

'For a few months now,' Sahni said, 'more and more people are rushing to join the daily parades of the Rashtriya Sevak Sangh. On top of that, they've also started getting trained in the use of weapons. Something to worry about, don't you think?'

'This Rashtriya Sevak Sangh has sprung up only recently,' said Sunder, 'but the Khalsas, Akalis and Nihangs have been parading for ages, decked out in their uniforms and equipped with swords and lances. That doesn't make any difference. What you need to be aware of is this: the riots have been going on in the country quite a while already, but no killing has taken place on religious grounds in Gobindpur or within a fifty-mile radius. And there won't be any.'

'Sunder Singh, how can you say that?' Sahni asked.

'Well, of course the riots will spread and reach villages and small towns like Gobindpur, as you say. But by that time, India will have been reduced to ashes by the fury of the blaze. Our political leaders, even if they know nothing else, must realize this and they'll put the breaks on the riots before that happens.'

'Yeah, sure, like they've got that much brains! The country is tottering on the brink of a blazing conflagration, the world is watching and waiting for it to keel over any moment, and at a moment like this Master Tara Singh makes a declaration of war, pouring oil on the fire. What a remarkable demonstration of intelligence! The leaders can jump-start the riots but they have no power to stop them. Once they start, riots have a mind of their own and take their own course.'

'Friends,' Ismail said, 'by the time it is proved which of your two theories is correct, I and the other Muslims of Gobindpur will already be in the next world. Over here, our immediate concern is how to survive, over there you two are busy explaining the independent psychology of the riots.'

Ismail's complaint provoked immediate silence. Sunder and Sahni realized they hadn't really given the dangers the Muslims of the town were facing the kind of weight that the present circumstances required. They also realized that their failure to put themselves in Ismail's place and look at the situation from his point of view was a sure sign of their immaturity. A lack of concern for the worries of others is a form of selfishness; only by overcoming such tendencies can people distinguish themselves from animals. In a way, this is perhaps the first step towards becoming human.

Finally Sunder spoke. 'The danger is definitely extreme, but it's not immediate. We still have some time. Sahni, let's go and see what's happening in the gurdwara and what those Rashtriya Sevak Sangh fellows are up to—what they're planning. Ismail, we'll be back by two. Don't worry. We're with you. We'll come up with some plan.'

After they left, Ismail came out into the street and stood there for some time, uncertain of himself. Then his feet began to move, as if on their own, towards the Muslim quarter. A crooked unpaved alley ran through a cluster of haphazardly built mud houses, with a stink-spewing drain in the middle that followed the serpentine course of the alley itself. Filthy water spilled out of it in many places and flowed into the alley. Weather-beaten, shapeless wooden doors, full of cracks, stood wide open, and children, without a stitch of clothing on their bodies, moved about freely in the courtyards, as usual. To Ismail, the quarter appeared to be wrapped in an ominous fog in which nothing could flourish except failure. And now, unbeknownst to its inhabitants, time had stretched a cloud of death over it. They still knew nothing about the swords hanging over their heads. 'O God,' Ismail entreated, 'will the stories told in the New Testament about the condemned communities which misfortune caught unawares be repeated again? But these are Muslims, God! They're innocent, poor, hard-working folks. Have pity on them, Lord.'

An echo resounded in his heart: 'Ismail, take a good look around you! Whoever fails to walk in step with the world is obliterated by the blowing sands of time. To maintain the balance.'

For a long time Ismail kept calling out to God, 'Why have

you forsaken us, Lord?' But this time no response echoed in his heart. Only the heavy, bluish, acrid smoke rising from the dung-cakes spread everywhere in the settlement stung his eyes, throat and palate. He could see women through the open doors as they rushed about in their courtyards with grimy dupattas thrown behind them on their backs and their faded worn-out clothes fluttering. Their continuous occupation with tasks as fruitless as that of the honeybees nearly made him cry. Despite such punishing labour, their hives remained empty of even one drop of honey. Why talk about honey or hives or bees when before long the very branch which was the site of all this intense activity would be lopped off!

There was a small piece of flatland beyond where the alley ended. Here, Baba Shahu had set up a loom by placing wooden stakes about four feet high in the shape of an X and stretching a nearly forty-foot-long warp thread over them. The two loose ends of the thread were tightly wound around the fat iron nails driven firmly into the ground. Holding a big heavy brush with tremendous difficulty, Baba moved it along the entire length of the warp and then back again. This back and forth would go on for hours. Such labour at his age! Ismail's heart overflowed with pity. He approached the man and said, 'Greetings, Baba-ji.'

'Greetings. May you live long!' Baba blessed him and stopped to look at him closely. His head and white-bearded face were unsteady. On his fair luminous forehead, partly hidden beneath his white turban, the black *mehrab*-shaped mark of piety went nicely with his low husky voice and mellow humble bearing.

'Son, I didn't recognize you. Which family are you from?'

'Sir, I'm Munshi Muhammad Din's son.'

'Muhammad Din? Wasn't he Kalu the teli's son?'

'Yes, sir.'

'Come close to me, my dear; let me give you my blessings. You're almost like my own grandson. Your grandfather, may God rest his soul, was a very close friend of mine. Kalu the oil presser and Shahu the weaver were known the world over for their arm-wrestling contests and for singing folk songs at fairs. The oil press that now belongs to Taja was originally yours. After Kalu's death your father sold the building, the oil press and the ox—everything—to his cousin Taja and went to live in the city. So tell me, have you too become some lawyer's scribe?'

'No, Baba. I'm still a student in Amritsar . . . in the fourteenth grade.'

'Bravo, bravo! So, you're going to become a big officer, then, eh? How did you happen to come this way today?'

'I came to see Uncle Taja for a bit.'

'Fine, fine. May you live long! This way we also got to see you. Taja is at home. I've just come from visiting him. And, yes, tell your father to come and show us his face some day. It seems he's angry with us, maybe more because of our poverty and ignorance than any other reason.' Saying this, Baba began applying the brush again. Ismail moved along.

Just past the flat piece of land, he found himself in another alley like the previous one. He hadn't gone far when he spotted Uncle Taja, who was ensconced on a cot, his blanket wrapped around him, absorbed in thinking and smoking his hubble-bubble. Tethered some distance from him on the opposite side was his ox, which looked even more contented than Taja himself, his eyes shut, quietly masticating. Inside the *kotha*, Taja's wife and her nine- or ten-year-old sister were hard at work cleaning the oil press, impervious, as it were, to the world around them. When his uncle saw him approach, he quickly made room for him on the cot and said, 'Come on, son. How are you? Come, sit.' He called, 'O Barkatay, come over here. See who's come.'

Barkatay appeared. She was a twenty-year-old woman, or maybe twenty-two, with a taut body and a complexion as sallow and fresh as the early morning—in other words, the youthful image of Punjabi womanhood. A heart still able to beat couldn't help feeling drawn to her alluring features, to the pull of her stunning body. The confidence with which she approached and then stood there left no doubt that she was conscious of her charm, and even more conscious of how relentlessly it worked. She wore silver studs in her ears. Her lips were hazel-brown from rubbing walnut bark and the gleaming white teeth between them looked like white jasmine buds. Her black dupatta had been thrown behind her on her back, and she had rolled her sleeves up to the elbows. Her hands and supple arms were smeared in oilcake, with drops of oil dripping from her hands. With pleasure mingled with surprise, she chirped as she saw Ismail, 'What a pleasant surprise! Our Babu is here! How lucky that you lost your way today and came hither! When did you get back from Ambarsar?'

'Three or four days ago.'

'Son, haven't you returned a little sooner than usual this time?' Taja asked.

'Yes, Chacha. The riots have started, so the government has closed all the schools and colleges in Punjab.'

'Damn these rioters. They've made living difficult for

everyone.' He looked towards Barkatay and said, 'But our Shida is still going to school these days, isn't he?'

'Dear God! Do you know anything about anything besides your ox and oil press? Shida doesn't go to a government school. He goes to study with the maulbi in the mosque.'

'Chachi, the girl who was cleaning the oil press with you—isn't she your oldest?' Ismail asked, a mischievous smile playing on his lips. She understood his joke. Feigning anger, she shot back, 'Come off it, you. Babbling away without knowing anything. Do I look that old to you? You know very well who she is. She's almost nine, while we've barely been married seven years. We have, may God guard him, only one child, Shida.'

'Chachi, get him admitted to the government school. When he passes grade four, then send him to the Khalsa School.'

'How is Sister Rajjo?'

'She's fine. She was cooking when I left.'

'She's forgotten us totally since she went to the city. Once she came back wearing a burqa and behaving very poised and reserved as if she was some queen. We all laughed at her. She never came back after that. Looks as though she was offended. Tell her to let it go. Everyone has forgotten about it. She may come back in her burqa a hundred times. No one will laugh at her again. She's given up visiting for no reason at all.'

Taja was feeling embarrassed that Barkatay had started talking in front of him about that incident with Ismail's mother. To change the topic he said, 'Will you go on talking forever or show Ismail some hospitality? Something to eat or drink?'

'Okay, I'll bring milk for him.'

'No, Chachi. I don't want milk. Just a glass of lassi with a pinch of salt will do.'

'But it's been so long since you were last here. Okay, I'll put some sugar in it.'

She smiled and turned with such coquetry that her silver studs swayed and her teeth sparkled brightly. The seductive attraction of his aunt's body and his own fear of succumbing to it made him cringe. 'It's not right that I like Chachi so much,' he thought with alarm.

As soon as she left, Ismail remembered why he had come there. To ensure secrecy he dropped his voice as he said, 'Chacha, there's no time to go on sleeping. Something must be done or else the Gobindpur Muslims will be slaughtered inside their houses.'

From Ismail's cautious tone, Taja had, in fact, got the hint to be circumspect, but he rejected the need for it. He attributed Ismail's effort to a mere lack of spunk, so he spoke irritably and loudly, 'Who would dare kill us? You think these Lalas would do that? Do they have the guts? Wouldn't I drink everyone's blood if they tried?'

'Calm down, Chacha! A little patience! This isn't the time for impetuousness. Let's try to understand the situation. This is not a fight between ten or twenty people in which one person's show of resolve might turn things around. It's a battle between two nations in which there are hundreds of thousands over here and the same number over there. Tara Singh, the leader of the Sikhs, has declared open war against the Muslims. The Lalas themselves won't have much to do with it. At most, they'll help the Sikhs with some money. You know there are Sikhs everywhere in Gobindpur. If a band of a few thousand pounces on you, what would you do, alone and empty-handed? Tell me that.'

'Have they done anything provocative yet?'

'How long does it take for something like that to start? There's still time. We'd better prepare ourselves.'

'I used to have a spear; don't know where it is now. The blade may even have become rusted.'

Hearing that, Ismail burst out laughing. He said, 'Chacha, we have to plan to save the mohalla in case of an attack, and nothing will be done without involving the residents. Surely the mohalla will provide the manpower, but we'll also need money to buy weapons. Let's do it this way. Tonight, I think I'll come back here after the Isha prayer. You ask seven or eight people from the mohalla to come over to your place. Let's consult with them before making any plans.'

'Yes, son. You're right.' This last statement, Taja, like Ismail, uttered in a hushed voice.

Initially, Tara Singh's declaration had no effect on the Sikhs of the area. Life in the town followed its usual peaceful course until early one morning Sunder Singh knocked on Ismail's door. 'Ismail,' he said, 'it looks as though things are beginning to get hot. Some Sikh leaders from Amritsar, Kapurthala and Lahore have been staying at the Khalsa School hostel since last night, and since the government has imposed a ban on public gatherings, they plan to give public speeches under the guise of kirtan. Men are being sent to the neighbouring villages to round up Sikhs. Prominent Sikh leaders have been holding meetings inside the hostel area since last evening. Nobody has a clue about what's cooking there, but we'll find out anyway, tomorrow, if not today. Things might get out of hand after the public meeting. An angry anguished mob might attack your house or overrun the Muslim mohalla. A rioting mob can do anything. I'm very worried about you.'

'Why do you worry so much, Sunder Singh? If that's how we're supposed to end, that's how it will be. What can we do?'

'Why don't you and your folks come over to our house?'

'And will this remain hidden? They'll discover it in no time at all. We have to die anyway; why put you through trouble and, in the bargain, bring destruction on your house? Let's wait and see how things evolve.'

At 3 p.m. Sunder came again and told him: 'The English deputy commissioner and the police captain managed to get there with an armed guard. I don't know how, through some stratagem I guess, they didn't allow the meeting to take place. All the visiting leaders were forced into a special lorry and sent away from Gobindpur. Catastrophe was at hand but has been averted. I think we should wait for the decision of the Boundary Commission. That will settle things down.'

'Who knows, the decision may take forever. We'll have died of fright by then.'

'Don't you worry, Ismail. We won't let you die like that. You're not alone. All the comrades in the area are with you.'

One evening Ismail's father said to him, 'Lala-ji is calling you. Go! See what he wants. He's in his office at the moment.'

'What does he want with me?'

'How do I know? Come on, get going. Remember, one day it will be from him that you'll learn to be a lawyer.'

He left for the Lala's office, which wasn't far, wondering what the man might want to tell him. He greeted him and took a chair. Lala-ji got up, shut the door, came back and sat down. Then he began talking cautiously. 'Son, I know that the lives of the Muslims in this area are in danger. It's good that as an educated young man you're aware of it. But in your inexperience you've ignored the fact that Gobindpur Muslims constitute only a very tiny minority, even less than the pinch of salt added to flour. What can a couple of hundred in a population of twenty thousand possibly do? If you think you can ensure their safety with handsaws and swords, you're completely wrong. And if a liberal-minded person like me, whom the sectarian Hindus consider their enemy just as much as they do the Muslims, has found out, without ever stepping out of his office, that you've started collecting weapons, you can expect everyone else in Gobindpur to know about it too. You're not planning on inciting the already enraged sectarians to attack you with the ruse of self-defence, are you? Now they're hell-bent on making you their first victim. My advice to you would be to leave Gobindpur immediately. Disappear in some big city until the situation has become normal again. Once you're gone, I'm sure the Congress-wallahs, the socialists, the peace-lovers and the humanists will bring the situation under control and enable the local Muslims to ride out this chaotic time in peace and quiet. I'll explain everything to your father. You just leave here quietly sometime tonight.'

Ismail was alarmed to hear all this. He went straight to Sunder Singh and Sahni. They decided that since it would be dangerous to travel by bus or train, they should avoid taking the paved roads and instead walk Ismail to Amritsar using the dirt track. They also thought it the better part of wisdom to give a wide berth to the bigger towns that lay along the way and not to enter any of the Muslim villages because of the potential danger posed by Singh's beard and long hair. Sahni was a frequent visitor to the villages in the area, where he had helped set up many farmers' organizations. Although he had not travelled to Amritsar on foot before, he was generally familiar with most of the paths and had peasant worker friends in the villages, who could easily set them up for the night. Ismail's name was changed to Balram; his real name was hidden even from Sahni's best friends. The distance to Amritsar was about eighty miles. The three of them set out the same night and arrived in Amritsar in four days. After leaving Ismail outside the Muslim mohalla of Sharifpura, Sahni and Singh turned back.

*

When Bashir reached home, the sun was about to set and, in the courtyard, the sparrows had already begun their descent into the thick foliage of the tall umbrella-shaped jujube tree for their nightly stay. They had struck up a deafening chorus. Bashir's wife and son sat on cots laid out in the water-sprinkled courtyard. On summer nights this was where they slept. Like the sparrows, they too were set for their nightly rest. The aroma of jasmine and moist earth was wafting all around, though it would be a while yet before the raat ki rani began to give off its fragrance. He enjoyed the incessant hullabaloo of the sparrows—which might have irritated another person overcome by the day's fatigue and oppressive heat—simply because it was his own home and the sound was a factor that made the house a home. Where else besides your own home could you find this feeling of affinity with your own being! It was another matter, though, whether self and home might both have their own secret regions that stay hidden from their owner.

The day's scorching heat, the restlessness of the journey and two days of being continuously knocked about in offices had taken their toll on Bashir. He was dejected, his shoulders slouching. After returning his greeting, his wife, seeing how immensely tired he looked, withheld the question that was on her lips, 'What happened?' Bashir sat on the cot and began taking off his shoes. He told his son to go to the drawing room, which also doubled as his office, and tell the scribe that he was back and would be there after his shower. When he emerged from the washroom after changing his clothes, his wife was waiting for him, sitting on the cot, ready with a tray of food. As he started to eat she finally did ask, 'So, were you able to accomplish anything?'

'Only the expected. We met all of them, the DC, the SP, the DIG and the home secretary, but they all repeated the same thing, "The AC and DSP present at the scene know the situation better and can better judge whether there is any danger to public peace. Come to us only after they've refused to listen to you."'

'Didn't you tell them that you've already met with them and that despite the dangerous conditions they're not willing to cancel the rally?'

'We did.'

'So?'

'So what? The same old tune: the officers present at the scene were responsible and reasonable. If they thought about it in a particular way, then that must be right.'

'In other words, they didn't cancel the rally?'

'No.'

'Will the organizers of the rally tell them after we're dead and gone that the Ahmadis were right after all? You should have pointed out that all the flyers have the DSP's name as the plaintiff. He's already joined our enemies. How can anyone expect fairness from him?'

'We did point that out.'

'Then?'

'They said that by being present at the scene, he'll be better able to observe the rally and ensure our security. His presence will prevent speakers from making inflammatory statements to the crowd. If a speaker does try that, he can stop him there and then.'

'And you agreed to it?'

'What else did you expect us to do? Did we have a choice?' he asked, a bit harshly.

'You had no choice? What does that mean? The lives of a handful of people surrounded by a majority gone wild . . .'

'Yes, yes, I know. If you think you could have presented our case so much better than Master Lateef and I could, why did you stay home? Why didn't you come with us?'

This time Amtul looked intently at Bashir's face, red with anguish, and then tears began to roll down her cheeks.

As he washed his hands Bashir thought: the people who had really caused his anger and irritation had been left behind in Lahore and its district offices, and here he was spilling out his anger on this poor woman who had been worried sick and whose anxiety had spurred on her passionate curiosity. He left for his office as soon as he had washed his hands.

Bashir's younger sister Nasira and two other women who lived on the same street, Masi Jannat and Taj Bibi, came in and sat down quietly near Amtul. They thought she would soon tell them herself how Master Lateef and Bashir's journey to Lahore had turned out. When she didn't speak for a long time, the visitors obviously assumed that the news wasn't good. But how bad? Bashir's sister couldn't hold back any longer and asked, 'Bhabi, was Brother Bashir able to make any headway in Lahore?'

'No. The big officers flat out refused to cancel the rally.'

'What?' they fearfully exclaimed in unison and then fell silent. Sounds from the street fused together into an interminable hum and pierced their numbed eardrums—a carefree guffaw or the catchy call of a pushcart vendor rising now and then in the discordant hum. The street was busy as always, yet here these women sat on cots, drowned in worry about themselves, and even more about the lives of their loved ones. A small boy sat on another cot a little distance away from them, his legs dangling, holding his chin in both hands, worrying about going to school again the next day and what might happen there. His heart fluttered continuously from the dread sweeping over the women's faces. He wasn't aware of the exact reason for his tremors, but he knew that the public rally in the city's grand mosque this coming Friday posed a serious danger to him, his family and all the residents of their street, and that it had particularly to do with their being Ahmadis. Would the organizers at the rally call them 'Mirzai dogs', as Dulla and Mehmand, his classmates at elementary school, had done? Would they swear at Hazrat Sahib and then laugh and make faces? Why would they do that? What quarrel did they have with Hazrat Sahib and with them? What had they done? He could never imagine that he and the other residents of the street might abandon Ahmadiyyat. He could never have done that because he considered Ahmadiyyat sacrosanct, as inevitable as his birth.

And it was the same for the rest of the denizens of the street, as natural as being born with a beating heart, two eyes, two ears and one nose. What could he and they do about it? To change his faith wasn't in his power, nor in the power of the residents of his street.

A full moon hiding behind the umbrella-like spread of the jujube tree was peeking through its foliage and laughing uproariously, scattering the laughter all around like a subtle shower of moonlight. Moonlight mixed with the pungent smell of raat ki rani, borne by the cool gentle breeze, spilled sweetly into the whole courtyard as a harbinger of life's beauty. But those four quiet women and the sad boy didn't notice it. They just drifted helplessly, each in their own torrent of fear. The boy, his heart overcome by the looming thought of persecution, began to cry, quietly for a while and then with sobs. He tried to throttle the sobs, but now and then one escaped. 'Someone seems to be crying somewhere,' Masi said.

The other women nodded as if Masi had spoken about something past and far away. Only after some time did it dawn on them that it was their own Mubashshir.

Amtul went over to him and gathered him in her arms. 'What's the matter, son? Why are you crying? What's happened?'

Barefoot, Nasira ran to the drawing room to get the boy's brother and knocked at the door.

'Poor boy,' Tajan said, 'he must have got scared.'

'In such fragrant moonlight, fairies and genies fly about,' Masi observed. 'Maybe some genie has affected him.'

Tajan said, 'Masi, the genie of the rally is more than enough for us. We don't need any other genie to scare the poor kid.'

Bashir opened the door and asked, 'What is it, Nasira?'

'Mubashshir is crying and won't quiet down. Won't tell us anything either. Have a look at him, please.'

Amtul briefly told him what had happened at school that day.

'Until now no one at school bothered him or any of our other kids on religious grounds,' Bashir remarked. 'The mere mention of the rally has started all this. The continuous speeches of the preacher have spread the poison of prejudice, even in the minds of the innocent children.' Bashir took the boy from Amtul and said to him, 'Son, the scourge of this rally will be over in a couple of days. After that, I'll take you to school myself. Don't worry. Everything will be all right. There's nothing to cry about. Tomorrow and the day after you're not going to school. All right?'

Bashir clasped his son to his breast and patted him, and the boy was a little comforted. The uneasiness about going to school was the one thing that had been conveyed to the others. Actually, Mubashshir had a pile of anxieties that had been gradually mounting the last few days—starting with the fingers pointing at him in the bazaar and the stony silent stares; the whispered conversations in faltering flighty words; the ashen perturbed faces of those near and dear to him; the broiling abhorrence and oozing malice of the long-bearded men in the street towards the stubbly growth on his father's chin; and the oppressive shrinking and narrowing of his immediate environment. If he shook off one layer of fear, another appeared in its place. Tired of the never-ending sequence, he looked at the faces of his mother, aunt and the other women for some comfort, but when he found them collapsing under the weight of despair, he too fell apart.

When the touch of his father's comforting hand on his back and the confident tone of his voice assured the boy that the danger was there but not severe or immediate, he fell asleep. As Bashir turned to go back to his office after laying the boy down in bed, Masi said, 'Bashir, son, listen for a moment to what I have to say.'

'Yes, Masi, what is it?'

'Son, you know, my Munawwar is addicted to wandering about. I cannot hold him back no matter how hard I try. I'm very scared of the wind that's blowing these days. Whenever he leaves home, I get worried sick. Everybody else is smart and canny. If there's a disturbance in the bazaar, they would know how to save themselves; what would that simpleton do? Do you think I should take him to Rabwah for a few days?'

'Masi, perhaps you should do that, but where will you stay in Rabwah?'

'In the guest house of the Jamaʿat Khana.'

'Look, Masi, just as there's this rally against us here, Lord knows, there may be many more going on in other places. As you already know, we're not allowed to recite either the *kalima* or even *bismillah*. If we do that, the police arrest us. It's a crime for us to say our prayers in someone's presence. Threats of murder have become a daily routine and these aren't just empty threats. People are really being killed. Every member of our community, at all times, everywhere, is a target of the terrorists. How many of us can the Rabwah people accommodate in the guest house? Disgusted by this permanent state of fear, many people have even left the country. But please don't worry. We're still trying to stop the rally. Even if we fail, we'll ensure everyone's safety and the safety of their property.'

In response, Masi of course said, 'All right, as you say; we won't go,' but her face suddenly fell. She held her forehead in her hands as if sunk in despair and began staring at the ground. She had thought that given Munawwar's disability, the situation called for a different course of action and that Bashir Ahmad hadn't given it proper consideration. If Bashir had given them a letter addressed to the in-charge of the guest house, he would surely have accommodated her and Munawwar. It was only a matter of a few days, anyway.

Amtul noted her anguish and quickly said, 'Masi, don't worry. We're all here with you. There's no cause for worry. By the grace of God Almighty, these days will pass without any incident. Keep on praying for His grace. Take care, though. For the next two or three days don't let Munawwar go out. If he's adamant, put him in a room and lock the door. Even if he cries, don't open the door.'

Noting how Amtul's comforting words had managed to pull the old lady out of the depths of her despair and how she acknowledged the constraints of the situation, Bashir said, 'Masi, you'll see, as soon as the gathering is over, everything will return to being as it was before. People won't even remember a word of, let alone be affected by, the heaps of falsehoods the speakers will have hurled at us. The "professionals" have created the whole situation. We can't blame them either; they rely for their bread and butter on the continuation of the unrest and having the state of mischief and discord prevail.'

Masi's real name was Jannat Bibi and she was about sixty-five. Even she didn't know exactly how old she was. Twenty years ago her husband, Chaudhry Naseer Ahmad, Bashir Ahmad's real uncle, passed away. Who awarded her the title

'Masi' and when and why, no one knew. The residents of the street were related to each other in one way or another, so everyone was connected to her through a variegated network of relationships. But everyone addressed her as Masi. Even her only son, Munawwar Ahmad, called her Masi. Unlike the other residents of the street, Masi wasn't born into an Ahmadi family. Many years before the partition of the country, when Naseer Ahmad had tied a *sehra* to his forehead and gone to her village with a big procession to marry her with great pomp and show, she and her parents didn't know that Naseer Ahmad and his parents were Ahmadis. And even if they had, by the time of the engagement or the wedding, it wouldn't have made any difference. They believed that Ahmadis were a sect of Islam like any other. However, if Naseer Ahmad had been found deficient by even a grain in being a Rajput, no relationship at all would have materialized between the two families. Even if that had happened by mistake and the mistake was discovered at the time of the wedding, as had been the case with Jannat Bibi and Naseer Ahmad regarding the Ahmadi connection, the wedding procession would have been sent back without the bride. The matchmaking relatives who knew Naseer was an Ahmadi treated it casually; they didn't even bother mentioning it to Masi's parents as something of particular importance. After the wedding, just as Masi accepted Naseer Ahmad, she also accepted the Ahmadi dispensation. This package deal wasn't meant for her family members, only for her; nor did her in-laws use her to put any pressure on her parents. So long as the elders in the bride's family were alive, the relations between both sets of in-laws remained warm and cordial and they socialized quite a bit. Her parental family even accepted the continuous proselytizing, which remained totally ineffective because they refused to add, modify or amend the faith they had inherited from their elders. Masi also went through the Ahmadi oath of fealty, for doing so would have been essential for her to keep peace in her household, to obtain Naseer Ahmad's love and to maintain her equality with the women among her in-laws. In her parents' house, religion had meant something needed to perform celebratory and mourning rituals, and in her new home, too, she continued to feel religion had about the same importance. She had also started saying her prayers, for it was an established practice in her father-in-law Gamey Khan's house, and she didn't wish to suffer belittlement. She did notice that there was greater emphasis on religion and its rites and rituals in her new family, which she sometimes felt went beyond necessary and reasonable limits, but she wasn't in a position to object to any of this, so she gradually became inured to it. In the matter of religion she refused to be involved in the troublesome business of asking questions about what, why and how: everyone, she believed, had to have some religion; so now that she had accepted Ahmadiyyat, she might as well follow it genuinely, and she was indeed doing it. However, she couldn't quite accept the tacit, verbally even unaccepted, but in practice quite effective custom of *peer-shahi* that went on in the hearts of the followers of Hazrat Sahib and his family. Of course, she did have respect for the women of the First Family, but never such devotion that, out of passionate intensity, she would roll at their feet and lick their soles. There was another difference as well: none of the venerable personages of her former religion was present in this world, whereas those of Ahmadiyyat were still alive. It is relatively easy to construct halos around great men who are dead since they only live in the thoughts of believers and don't return to the world in flesh and blood. Their halos can only grow more brilliant with time, not lessen in their splendour. To conceive of a human being who is present before your eyes as 'light upon light' isn't easy. Feelings of envy, jealousy and rage inevitably intervene. When devotion is subjected to the crucible of these feelings, it often emerges at the other end in strange, laughable forms. This was how Masi thought about the issue: religiously these people might well enjoy a lofty position, but they were no Rajputs. They belonged to other castes. In her view, no caste could be more elevated than the Rajputs. Naseer Ahmad might well show them great respect and regard—that was his business. But he had a higher station than they did; firstly, because he was a Rajput, and secondly, because he was her husband.

When the country was partitioned, she had observed how the oppressive conduct of the majority had forced them to leave their homes, their belongings and the graves of their ancestors, and move over to this side. Now they were facing another majority, of their own kind, which was forcing them to give up their faith or their lives would be made impossible for them. Why should she do that? she exclaimed in her heart. More than faith, it had now become a matter of pride for her. Then again, she considered it her birthright to ensure the safety of her feeble-minded son and herself in whatever way possible. Masi did indeed have many children born to her, but they had all died in infancy. Munawwar was the only one who survived and he was now nearing thirty—over six feet tall, but in mental abilities no different from a three-year-old. Early in the morning, Masi would send him out in a suit of clothes freshly laundered by a washerman, but when he returned his clothes would be wretchedly filthy. He would never make any change in the way she dressed him. If she buttoned the top button of his shirt, he wouldn't open it no matter how hot or stuffy it felt. In the winter, if she inadvertently left the collar of his jacket upturned, upturned it remained the whole day. If anybody else tried to fix it, he wouldn't let them touch it, saying, 'No, no, Masi would beat me up.' For every job he didn't want to do, he would use the same excuse. Actually, the poor woman didn't even utter a harsh word to him in anger, let alone beat him. His sagging body had the plumpness of a suckling babe. With his flabby stomach, slouched shoulders and stooping neck, he would wander about the alleys and bazaar lost in his thoughts. Whether it was a monkey show or some juggler performing tricks, a crowd gathered to buy tooth powder or potency pills, Munawwar was sure to be there. Masi purposely had him sport a short, light, French-cut beard so that in every which way he would appear to be an offspring of the Chaudhry family. She wanted everyone in Sultanpur to remember that Munawwar belonged to that family so that, after her own death, if Bashir Ahmad ever turned dishonest and didn't give Munawwar his share from the profit of his ancestral land, at least there would be people to sympathize with Munawwar's pitiable condition and take Bashir Ahmad to task for his conduct. What would happen after Munawwar died—she couldn't allow her thoughts to stretch that far. The management of Munawwar's land was in Bashir Ahmad's hands. Of its income he would regularly remit ten per cent every month, with her permission, to Rabwah, and hand over the rest to her with the breakdown written on a slip of paper. Bashir Ahmad was a scrupulously honest man and Masi expressed complete trust in him. She never counted the money—at least not in Bashir Ahmad's presence—and she always returned the slip of paper to him there and then rather than holding on to it herself. Given the circumstances, this was the proper conduct. Every shopkeeper of the city, indeed every resident, knew and recognized Munawwar. When he got tired of wandering, he just sat himself down on the stoop of any shop he happened to notice first. The shopkeepers laughed and joked with him, and he laughed with them, without understanding the jokes, and talked with them innocently just like the kids. If anyone offered him tea or water, he would drink it. He never asked for anything himself, nor bothered anyone. People found him very endearing. If some kids tried to tease him, they would be scolded away. Some credulous people elevated him to the level of a saint. Some gamblers haunted him, hoping he might reveal the winning numbers to them. When he felt hungry, he just got up and walked home. Sometimes he would go to Ismail's shop. Lovingly, Ismail would make him sit down in a chair and always say the same thing: 'Come! How are you, the innocent member of the family of the wise? Come along.'

With a somewhat silly smile he would sit down and look around sheepishly, too shy to meet Ismail's eyes.

'Munawwar, son, listen. Never give Masi any trouble. Your paradise is under her feet. You'll never find such comfortable shade anywhere else in the world.'

'Masi good.' And then he would lift the end of his shirt and spread it towards Ismail, and the latter would say, 'Yes, it's a very fine shirt. Who gave it to you?'

There was pride and a sense of belonging on his face: 'Masi!'

After Munawwar left, Ismail heaved a stoic sigh and exclaimed, 'I wonder why God allowed him to be born into the family of such wise and intelligent people? As a punishment for them or a lesson for others?'

Taj Bibi, the woman who had come along with Masi, was about thirty-five. It was the first time in three years that she had set foot in Amtul's house. She wouldn't have come even today had it not been for some pressing questions that needed quick answers. Some evil forebodings were bothering her; a vague trepidation was eating her up from within—what's going to happen? It was no longer just a personal question; it was a palpable dread, a wavering dread, that hung everywhere in the air and put her nerves on edge. It was night-time and her husband hadn't returned home. Lord knows where he'd gotten stuck. If he were home, she would have sent him instead. Now, weighed down by her own worries and desperately needing to find some comfort, she'd come to see Masi. As soon as she came in, she fired off the question, 'What news have Brother Bashir Ahmad and Master Lateef brought from Lahore?'

'Tajan, sit down first. I'll tell you, Bibi. Everyone knows they've returned, but not what they have accomplished there, at least not yet.'

'All right, tell me, is the meeting still on?'

'It isn't clear yet.'

'If it is, what will become of us? They might attack us.'

Masi said, 'Listen, Tajan, what you want to know can only be found out from where you're loath to go. Come on, let's go to Nasira's house. If we don't get the answers there, we'll go to Amtul's. You don't have a feud with her, do you?'

Tajan uttered a longish 'No,' and then added, 'hardly.'

More than those two words, her tone and the cadence of her voice betrayed her true feelings: an assertion of her benevolence—as if saying, 'We don't hold grudges very long, even against our enemies'; a muted admission of anguish, a complaint about the pressure of unfavourable circumstances; and, in between, a mild note of having acted against her will in deciding to go. Tajan stood up and followed Masi slowly. Fear was now driving her where, under normal circumstances, she would never have considered going.

There was a time when Amtul and Tajan had a great friendship. And even now they weren't involved in open warfare; only a limited, private cold war was raging between them. The neighbourhood women knew about it, though none of the men did; and even if they did, they couldn't care less about the squabbles among the women. The matter was simply that Taj Bibi had asked for the hand of Amtul's younger sister who was studying for a master's degree, for her younger brother, a high-school graduate and a *patwari* who owned six or seven acres of land in Noor Nagar village. Instead of treating this proposal as something she would look at sympathetically, Amtul felt rather offended. She didn't say anything, just waved her hand contemptuously in rejection and turned her face the other way. Finally, when she did speak, all she said was, 'Was a patwari the only man left for my beautiful educated sister?' Tajan felt so small that she didn't know where to hide. This exchange pretty much ended their relationship. However, Taj Bibi took no small pleasure now from the fact that Amtul's sister, nearing thirty, was still a spinster and a teacher in a girls' college, while her brother was happily married and had even fathered a son.

What had prompted Tajan to ask for the match was that her brother combined three qualities that were hard to come by in an eligible suitor: he was a Rajput, he was educated and he was an Ahmadi. She would tell herself confidently, 'Let's see how she finds an Ahmadi, a Rajput and an educated one at that, for her sister. I bet her sister will remain a spinster all her life and die pining for a husband. Go ahead, enjoy your master's degree, hunh!'

In the meanwhile, three or four neighbourhood women with half a dozen of their kids in tow walked hesitantly into the courtyard. Soon a few more women came in. A veritable crowd of women and children gathered. Cots and just about anything one could sit on were dragged out of the rooms into the courtyard. A throng of women was sitting there, all holding their breath. Even the kids weren't arguing. They sat hushed, overcome by fear, as if they'd been earmarked for the slaughterhouse and were awaiting their turn to be called in. The sound of Bashir Ahmad talking softly came wafting in from the drawing room like a distant hum, interrupted now and then by a louder voice, and then a jumble of three or four voices, after which the same continuous hum of Bashir Ahmad's voice. Despite the heat, they had shut the windows and doors, and were talking in hushed tones, so only a low jingling reached the women sitting in the courtyard. From the rise and fall of the voices, they could, to some extent, surmise the significance of the subject under discussion. Training their ears on the sounds, they tried their best to catch some strand of the conversation but failed. Once when Nasira tiptoed to the door and put her ear to it, she could hear Malik Muhammad Rafiq talking. She recognized his voice immediately but couldn't catch what he was saying. She had been to Rafiq's house many times, a spacious home adjacent to a street near the main bazaar. Rafiq also came from Ismail's ancestral village of Gobindpur and was a member of his extended family. He converted to the Ahmadi faith well before Partition, while he was working as an overseer at the Delhi Municipal Committee. He had two daughters and two sons, all of whom were close to finishing their education. They were a very sincere Ahmadi family. The older son, after doing his master's degree, had devoted his life to the jamaʿat, and was now the head of its Mission in Nigeria. When the second son, Nasr, did his medical degree, Malik Rafiq sought to marry him to Nasira. She knew the young man quite well and even liked him. After she started wearing niqab, a bashful smile spread across their lips whenever their eyes met, despite the veil, and the effect of such perfunctory encounters left her in a dazed state for days. At Malik Rafiq's constant prodding, Bashir Ahmad fearfully submitted this proposal to his father, Chaudhry ʿAta Muhammad. Chaudhry sahib suddenly became incensed. He stood up and said, 'Bashir Ahmad, what are you saying? Have you lost your senses? They may be Ahmadis a hundred times over, but I cannot marry my daughter into a family of the oil-pressing caste. You should have thought of this yourself before talking to me.' Nasr went to the United States, did his MD, married a white woman and settled there. He'd been gone for five years. Meanwhile, Nasira was married off to one of her cousins, the son of her maternal aunt and an inspector in the excise department. She seemed to have no complaints about her married life, but if by any chance, as now, the thought of Nasr wandered into her heart, a resigned sigh did not fail to escape from her lips.

Nasira put her ear to the door once again and tried to

listen while the women fixed their gaze on her. This time it was Munir Ahmad talking, but she still failed to catch the drift of his talk. She looked at the women and, pointing towards her ear, shook her hand in the negative. Nasira was young, a graduate and the product of the new age. She was constantly aware that whenever the sectarian balance in society went out of kilter, women were affected by it as much as men. They suffered fear and worry, and were as afraid of death as the men. In fact, they faced the added burden of keeping the children safe as well as worrying about protecting their own honour. And yet, even those among them who had sound judgement were never taken into confidence; they were only informed of the decisions made by their menfolk. It was a man's world, and all religions, in spite of their claim to adhere to the ideals of justice and equality, in fact took an identical path in the matter, her own being no different. At this point she had to rein in her thinking because she'd been taught that issues already settled by religion should not be made contentious. Opening them up to questioning would only lead her to the doorstep of apostasy. Grudgingly, she submitted to the privilege of men in making decisions.

Frightened at seeing the pale and haggard faces of their mothers, the children tried hard to push up against their sides, as if wanting to backtrack into their mothers' wombs. The women were not privy to the individual thoughts and views of the local Ahmadi elders—those empowered to make decisions—about these issues, but everyone knew which matters needed to be decided. They had all been there for two hours already, waiting to hear the decisions. On the surface, they were steadfast and sat quietly and patiently, but their taut nerves were just about ready to snap. Had Bashir Ahmad not emerged soon after, some of them, overcome by the suspense and the suffocating smell of each other's perspiration, would have started beating up their children, or, using the pretext of the heat, gotten into a turf war with women sitting too close to them, or loudly cursed the organizers of the Friday rally.

Initially, Bashir Ahmad was taken aback seeing the crowd of women and children in his courtyard. Then he realized that these poor women had also been under severe mental pressure for the past few days. They had assembled there because, alone, they couldn't have continued to endure this state of uncertainty in which the question of life and death had become entangled. To live in constant fear of death—one's own, and those of one's children, one's husband and relatives—was a torment exhausting enough to crack the toughest among them. Bashir Ahmad appeared calm. He spoke in a steady voice that dispensed assurance to one and all. 'Sisters, there's nothing to be worried about; by God's grace everything is going well and will even end, God willing, in the right way. Some of us will go again tomorrow to see the authorities. Even if they refuse to cancel the rally, it won't matter. Let the rally take place; we'll arrange for our own security as we deem fit. It's not easy for anyone to attack this street. We're doing what we can to ensure our safety. You need two hands to clap and we'll never become the hand that joins the other in clapping. We haven't harmed anyone, why would anyone come to harm us?

'The good Lord has His mysterious ways to help the oppressed. Count on His grace and forgiveness. Now please go home and sleep peacefully. May the Lord support and protect you.'

The women started leaving one by one. When Taj Bibi was about to go, Amtul said, 'Bhabi, please come over sometimes. It would be relaxing. I've been thinking of visiting you for quite some time now, but these household chores—they never seem to end. Let the trouble of the rally pass and I'll come by.'

'Sure, do. Sister, come a hundred times. My house is like your own house.'

Although the collapsing spirits received a little ballast from Bashir Ahmad's speech, a nagging doubt still lingered. As suggested by the other members of the group, Bashir Ahmad had deliberately refrained from letting the women in on two important decisions made that evening. This would have made things worse for the ones already frightened and the order and discipline that had until now held that small group together would have snapped. That order and discipline were now the sole guarantee of the group's safety since the government agencies responsible for public safety, even if not actually in cahoots with the other side, had at best remained aloof. The decisions Bashir Ahmad had withheld were as follows: Firstly, on the day of the rally, before the second watch, six Ahmadi households settled in other areas of Sultanpur would quietly leave town. And, secondly, in the event of an attack and the failure of the strong iron gate (put up by the non-Muslim residents of the street for their own security and still in good working order) to stop a formidable number of attackers from storming in, the street's residents would lock their houses from the inside, walk through the interconnecting doors to the last house, go out into the fields and from there walk to Noor Nagar, Munir's village. Every household in Noor Nagar owned some agricultural land and Ahmadis were in the majority.

Even non-Ahmadis were somehow related to them. No non-Ahmadi landlord, with the exception of Sarfaraz Husain, was likely to deny them protection.

Munir Ahmad owned fifty acres in Noor Nagar. Since the landholdings in the area had continuously become smaller due to successive divisions of properties, even an owner of fifty acres was considered a better-than-average landholder. Taking full advantage of his BSc degree in agriculture, Munir Ahmad had begun farming with scientific know-how and was quite successful. In order to meet the professional demands of his enterprise as laid down in the books, he, in fact, kept his permanent residence in the village on the land itself. He was a hard-working man, disciplined, of regular habits, and a progressive farmer who immersed himself in his work. He had no interest in legal disputes, running around to the courts and police stations, or in any of the other customary activities with which landowners occupied themselves. His only misfortune was that his land was adjacent to that of Sarfaraz Husain. Sarfaraz belonged to the same caste as Munir. The elders of both had come from the same village in eastern Punjab in 1947 and settled in Noor Nagar. Sarfaraz had only a modest education and the mentality of a traditional landowner. He was himself a rogue and had befriended the other rogues in the area. Bribing revenue and police officers, and often working for them as their agent, was for him a means to solidify relations with them and earn some extra income. His landholding was close to a hundred acres. He didn't hesitate to use any means, no matter how low or criminal, to achieve his objective. In the past, other than a mutual dislike, there was no animosity between Sarfaraz and Munir. Not so now. Sarfaraz had contacts in the administrative office of the local police, from the deputy superintendent down to the ordinary policemen. Ever since the present deputy had arrived, Sarfaraz had become a tad more arrogant because the deputy wasn't just dishonest, he was downright dissolute. He often came to Sarfaraz's *dera* to have some fun.

Part of Munir's land, a two-acre triangle, was wedged into Sarfaraz's property. A few years ago, Munir planted a guava and orange orchard on the land, which had now started producing a good yield of fruit. As the water from the canal was insufficient for his other twenty-five acres of orchard, Munir also installed a tube well on the same two acres. Sarfaraz was intent on grabbing that piece of land cheaply by any means possible, even bullying and coercion, because in his eyes it was an ideal place to set up a new dera for himself. Many times Sarfaraz had sent his scribe and made an offer to buy that land, but each time Munir had declined politely. One day Sarfaraz walked over to Munir's dera in person with the same proposal, but Munir skirted the issue. Before the current DSP came along, Sarfaraz had made an attempt to take over the desired land by force, with the help of his ruffian friends. His idea was to file a civil suit claiming that Munir Ahmad had sold the land to him, handed over the deed and received full payment, but was now dilly-dallying about the transfer of the property. He planned to request the registrar to issue the registration of the land in his name, but Munir, with the help of his friends and servants, soundly thwarted the attempt. Even though Munir did manage to rout Sarfaraz's scheme, a servant and one of his friends received injuries in the ensuing scuffle. One of them was injured so seriously that he had to spend a number of days in the hospital. After some running around, and taking advantage of Bashir Ahmad's professional acumen and wide contacts, Munir was able to file an FIR (First Information Report) with the police against Sarfaraz and his companions, which had now been under investigation for a whole year in the court of the local magistrate. The Ahmadis in the village had sided with Munir, not only because he was in the right, but also because he was an Ahmadi, while his opponent was not. According to the FIR, the majority of the witnesses for the plaintiff belonged to the Ahmadi sect. When the new DSP arrived he tried, with the help of some influential landholders in the area, to put some pressure on Munir Ahmad to withdraw the FIR and do a deed of compromise, but Munir refused to oblige.

The deputy was terribly annoyed by Munir's refusal to yield. He decided to teach him a lesson, and not just him but also Bashir Ahmad in particular and the whole Ahmadi community of the area in general. He thought up a plan—one tried before by many others in different places—to take the staunch active opponents of the Ahmadis into his confidence and stir up a movement against them. He first sent Sarfaraz to sound them out. When they expressed a willingness, he met them himself and assured them of every kind of help and support. The rally was then announced; huge posters were put up not only in Sultanpur but also in adjoining areas. Well-known speakers from far and near agreed to come. The invitees from the nearby towns not only promised to come, they also promised to bring along large numbers of students from religious madrassas. After the announcement of the rally, even though on the surface life in Sultanpur remained calm, below the surface, on a level hidden from sight, a commotion had begun to stir. The attitude of the people towards Ahmadis remained normal, but in the pond of their unarticulated thoughts about Ahmadiyyat, it was as if a stone had suddenly plopped. After giving the matter some thought, they concluded: Ahmadis must be up to something against us, that's why every other day there's this outcry against them. It's true enough that Ahmadi beliefs are different from ours; it's also true that the government's attitude towards them during the past thirty years has been harsh and unjust, not one of equality. All the same, it's possible that out of anger or a desire for revenge, Ahmadis have done things contrary to the interests of our country and religion that we haven't discovered due to our simple-mindedness and lack of time. Perhaps the people who are responsible for keeping themselves informed about the activities of the Ahmadis know what the Ahmadis have done? Now, on the day of the rally, their speeches will reveal what new information they've dug up.

Common folk had no inkling that two acres of land between Munir and Sarfaraz was the real cause of the trouble, and that Sarfaraz and his companions were manufacturing sectarian strife to punish Munir and the other Ahmadis. The spreaders of prejudice weren't motivated by any principle or ideology; they were using deception to provoke gullible people and exploit them for their own goals, although the people had no reason to suspect all that. The mature ones among them felt that, however wrong and damaging to the country the views of the spreaders of prejudice might be, at least they firmly believed those views to be true enough to promote them. If only they realized that bigots have no honesty, not even a grain of it, and they wittingly make falsehood appear to be truth.

One Friday before the rally, a lengthy speech was delivered in the main mosque of Sultanpur (the same venue where the rally was to take place) to prove that Ahmadiyyat was a menace to Islam. There was nothing new in the speech; the same recital of old objections was being heard again after many years. The speech only stirred up the old strife that had long lain dead for the public. It was the kind of snake that could devour you if you weren't level-headed. At first, the speech frightened the audience, but the sensation proved to be short-lived. It soon exited their minds, for, in reality, there was no impending danger anywhere. Perhaps they figured out that the snake was made of cardboard. As they filed out of the mosque, no one said anything about it; they'd already forgotten everything. They went home merrily talking and laughing among themselves. Once an audience has moved out of the range of such a harangue, it's hard for them to be persuaded to engage in violence.

When frightened, animals and humans react the same way: if the enemy is strong, they take to their heels; if weak, they stand their ground and do battle. Why wouldn't a majority, especially one so overwhelming, be ready to kill and be killed? Magnanimity alone—something we sorely lack as a nation—holds back violence, even when one has the strength to annihilate the other. Had the speaker wanted, he could have easily sent the audience to storm the Ahmadis in their homes. But that, of course, was not part of the prearranged plan. The speech was instead meant to introduce the audience, ahead of the forthcoming rally, to its subject matter.

As the fateful day drew near, the Ahmadi minority became more nervous and perturbed about securing its life, property and honour, while the majority continued to engage in its preoccupations free of care, totally unconcerned about the plight of the minority. During the intervening days, if the mind of someone of the majority wandered off thinking about the rally, it was merely a fleeting thought: would the anticipated drama provide the expected sensation, or would it lose steam and fade away even before that?

Sarfaraz Husain, perfectly content in his village, continued with his daily chores as if he didn't know what was about to happen. He'd paid the sum demanded by the deputy sahib for arranging the revenge which his enemies weren't likely to forget for generations, and now he sat waiting for the show to begin, outwardly at peace but inwardly restless. He was afraid of failure, which could happen only if the officials at the provincial level interfered. That they had refused to do so was a piece of news that hadn't reached him yet. To gain a trifling advantage and to punish Munir Ahmad for stubbornly hanging on to his legitimate rights, he'd set the wheel of oppression in motion in such a way that three hundred innocent people of Sultanpur and Noor Nagar had been seized for a whole week by the unremitting fear of being slaughtered by the majority, while he himself sat back, relishing their awful plight. He felt he was getting his revenge. The majority was unconcerned anyway. Two jobs assigned to him had yet to be carried out. Firstly, on the night between Wednesday and Thursday he was supposed to have his men burn some pages of the Holy Qur'an, scatter them inside the Ahmadis' place of worship, and then raise a caterwaul that the Ahmadis had disgraced the Qur'an. And secondly, a day before the rally, he was to have the Ahmadi households marked with a designated chalk sign so the out-of-town attackers did not mistakenly damage the life and property of anyone else. His collaborator, the DSP, had purposely left town for a tour of the area so there was no possibility of any blame falling on him. He was expected to return the evening before the rally.

The students of the madrassa of the congregational mosque were busy arranging for food and lodging for the out-of-town speakers and for students from the nearby religious schools, a great number of whom had been invited to participate. On explicit instructions from their bosses, the staff of the local tycoons and industrialists were helping the students as volunteers. None of the elected government officials or the members of the Opposition or of any political party had attempted to come to Sultanpur to stop the imminent disturbance, to comfort the troubled and distressed Ahmadis, to draw the attention of the officials responsible for preserving public peace to the gravity of the situation, or to persuade them to take the necessary steps. Since by law they were not going to get the votes of the Ahmadis, it was most unlikely any officials would come out to support them. Then there were those who had voted for them or had someone cast their vote on their behalf. The authorities could ill afford to alienate them and earn their animosity. Politics had always been a game of give and take. As a minority, the Ahmadis had the right to have two of their members elected to the National Assembly. However, no Ahmadi ever contested those seats. And if anyone defied the clear policy of the jamaʿat and did contest the seats, no other Ahmadi attached any significance to whether or not the candidate was elected unopposed. Ever since this law was enacted, the Ahmadis had considered it downright prejudicial and reacted by totally boycotting the electoral contests for the two seats reserved for their sect. It was also said that the leaders of the anti-Ahmadi movement throughout the country enjoyed the secret patronage and silent support of the government. The officials had been issued instructions accordingly. The government's rationale was this: if by sacrificing a few dozen Ahmadis it could show favour to the national leadership of the anti-Ahmadi movement, it could easily extract big concessions from them in return in the future. Not a bad bargain at all. And, besides, it was the safest way of sacrificing Ahmadis: no outcry at the public level; no protest marches; no whining or wailing in the newspapers; no damage to the vote bank, if anything, a chance to augment it further. What difference would it make if in the surging sea of the majority, fifty or sixty dead bodies and as many houses with their belongings were offered up? Why, none at all. The briefly scattered surface would again patch up and blend, as if nothing had happened.

On Wednesday morning at seven, Chaudhry Bashir Ahmad, Master Lateef, Munir Ahmad and Malik Muhammad Rafiq gathered to meet the assistant commissioner by the road outside his bungalow, as they had planned the night before. At that time, in their anxiety and bewilderment, and under tremendous mental pressure to meet him as quickly as possible, they had overlooked the need to set up a prior appointment with him, considering it irrelevant. Now, after the night's rest that had cleared their thinking and calmed their minds, each of them independently was convinced that further meetings with the assistant commissioner and the deputy superintendent would not produce any result. Nothing was to be gained by such meetings. The officials had pre-planned their moves based on their own objectives, not on any thought for the safety of the Ahmadis, and would act according to those objectives. No arguments or appeals from any Ahmadis would change the established priorities.

The bungalow was situated outside the city on the road to Lahore. Now and then a bus hurtled by, raising a cloud of dust. Everywhere, as far as the eye could see, green crops glinted in golden sunshine. The green leaves of the huge plump trees at the edge of the road and around the vast lawn of the bungalow stirred and swayed gently in the early morning breeze. The four visitors, each lost in his own thoughts, stood impervious to their surroundings. The gun-toting sentinel standing guard at the gate of the bungalow told them, 'Sahib's gone for a walk. He'll be back soon. Go inside and have a seat over on the lawn.' As they moved towards the lawn, Munir just seemed to have had enough and blurted out, 'The AC has no interest in our concerns, let alone any sympathy, don't we know that already? He's not going to do anything for our security. We'll have to do whatever needs to be done by ourselves. Let's go back.'

'There's such a thing as going by the book, which also has value,' Bashir Ahmad remarked. 'God forbid, if something unpleasant happened tomorrow, they at least won't be able to blame us for not having alerted them in time to find some remedy.'

Munir said, 'Brother, the "going by the book" has already been done. We've warned them of the danger. What more do we need to say to hear from them? The AC couldn't even stop the DSP from chairing a session of the rally. What more can he do? You've met the provincial officials in Lahore, told them about the whole situation, but no one has done anything. Have they? You've even met this fellow once before, and told him everything in detail. Is anything left undone? It seems to me the whole administration, from here to Lahore, is hell-bent on getting us lynched. I don't know what they really want. Maybe it'll become evident in a few days. Come on, let's go back.'

Malik Rafiq said, 'Munir Ahmad, you're still young and a bit impetuous. Have some patience. What other option do we have except asking for the administration's help and cooperation? What we could decide on our own, we did last night. That doesn't need to be changed.'

'Many other options are still open to us, Malik sahib!' Munir said somewhat testily, getting red in the face. 'Don't even worry about Noor Nagar. No one will dare trouble us there. As for Brother Bashir's street in Sultanpur, if the gate is shut and two people with guns stand guard, even a crowd of ten thousand wouldn't be able to take a step forward. Take my word for it! You won't even need to fire a shot.'

Master Lateef was getting upset. He said, 'Chaudhry Munir, you haven't lost your mind, have you? If we so much as hold a firecracker in our hands, let alone a gun, it would be like dropping an atomic bomb on the three million Ahmadis in this country. I hope you're not opening the path to genocide?'

Munir responded, 'Well then, do what you will. I'll have nothing to say.'

'Keep your spirits up, Chaudhry Munir,' Malik Rafiq said. 'Even if the rally does take place, nothing untoward will happen. Everything will be fine, by God's grace. At worst, some of our houses might be looted; one or two may even be torched. A half-dozen of our men might be hurt; one or two might even lose their lives. You've chosen to follow the path of righteousness; there will be many occasions that will call for the sacrifice of blood and life.'

Laughing, Bashir Ahmad added, 'Yes, these things do happen in this business.'

The AC, a middle-aged man, had started out with the assistant tehsildar's job and risen to his current position. Kowtowing to his seniors was his special quality, and he regarded his present position as a reward for it. He walked through the gate twirling his cane and came straight towards them. With knitted brows he said to Bashir Ahmad, 'What can I do for you, gentlemen?'

'We've come to resubmit our concerns regarding the rally and to bring to your attention some new misgivings we have about it.'

'This is neither the time nor the place for it. Come to my office.' He uttered his words with considerable annoyance. All four felt humiliated and began to walk out. If Bashir Ahmad weren't such a popular and well-known lawyer, they wondered how insulting the AC's attitude would have been. As they were leaving, Malik Rafiq seemed to be thinking out loud: two hundred people are facing death night and day, and this fellow can only think about the appropriate time and place!

On arriving at the AC's office at ten o'clock, Bashir Ahmad found out that the AC was hearing cases at the moment and wouldn't be free before one o'clock. He sat down in the courtroom in one of the lawyers' chairs to wait for the AC, hoping that he might eventually catch the fellow's attention. Half an hour later, the AC asked him, 'Chaudhry sahib, what brings you here?'

'I need an appointment to see you, sir.'

'Come to my office at three.'

At three Bashir Ahmad went to the AC's office with his three companions. As soon as he entered, the AC asked, 'Chaudhry sahib, any incidents anywhere?'

'No, sir, not so far. It's to forestall just such an eventuality that we've been bothering you time and again.'

'Aren't you a bit more hypersensitive than need be? Be patient. Nothing is going to happen. The number of police on duty is more than adequate to control the crowds at the rally. And, if the need arises, we can always call in additional forces on short notice from other nearby police stations and from the provincial capital. I've talked to the officials who are in charge and everything is settled. Both the DSP and I have spoken to the local leaders of the movement. They've assured us that public peace will not be disturbed, nor will the Ahmadis be harmed in any way. I think this should satisfy you.'

'Sir,' Muhammad Rafiq began, 'we appreciate your attention in this matter. It guarantees the safety of both our lives and our property, and we're grateful to you for it. However, what usually happens on such occasions is that while the leaders talk about the difference in our faiths in their speeches, they also pile on us, at the same time, baseless and totally fabricated accusations regarding the safety and security of the country and the safeguarding of its interests. This inflames the public who really begin to consider us the enemy. The crowd, without any leader's inducement or guidance, gets out of control and assails our houses. That needs to be taken care of.'

'If you're asking me to ban the rally, that won't happen,' the AC responded firmly. 'I remember explaining to you even in the previous meeting that every sect in our country has the right to propagate and communicate its beliefs in a peaceful manner. There's no tension in Sultanpur and there's no danger to public peace; so there's no justification for imposing Section 144. We've already discussed with the leaders the issues they intend to talk about in their speeches. They've assured us with God as their witness that they will not say or do anything that might provoke sectarianism. If they flout this agreement, they'll both lose our trust in the future and will be punished for breaking their promise. We also have other means to punish them, and they know these well. They won't dare break their promise.'

'But, sir,' Master Lateef started, 'our biggest worry is that when earlier incidents of arson, pillage and murder occurred on a large scale against the Ahmadis at the hands of the inflamed public, they all started exactly the same way as we see developing today. In almost every case, first a dispute between an Ahmadi and a non-Ahmadi arose over a house or a piece of land, and when the non-Ahmadi couldn't legally get his way, he used his influence and money to turn the issue into an anti-Ahmadi movement. The ordinary man is just used as an instrument and doesn't even know that a dispute over property is the real reason behind the movement. Seized by passion, he commits or is made to commit atrocities against innocents to safeguard the sanctity of his faith. In this instance, too, an unpleasantness over a piece of land between Munir Ahmad and Sarfaraz Husain has turned into a rally against the Ahmadis. When the beginnings look the same, one is scared about the endings.'

'Look,' the AC began, 'this is just your speculation. It's hard to accept until we've obtained investigative reports on all such riots and thoroughly compared them, but one thing is quite certain: the responsibility for all these incidents and rallies that keep taking place all the time throughout the country lies squarely on you. Both the law and the Constitution have declared Ahmadis non-Muslims, but you haven't accepted this status—neither inwardly, nor in practice. If you accepted it and then realistically determined your status and place in society for what they are, we would all be spared this daily misery, you and us.'

'That indeed is a lengthy discussion and unrelated to the issue at hand,' Bashir Ahmad replied. 'Nevertheless, when you have the time, we shall discuss it. Noor Nagar is three and a half kilometres away. After the rally, it is unlikely that the excited mob will reach there still in their heightened state of emotion. And even if some do reach there, they may find it difficult to maintain their agitation. Then again, Ahmadis are a majority of those living in Noor Nagar, so, we believe, they will be safe there. There haven't been any signs of danger there either, at least not so far. On Friday, just for that one day, if you could post some armed policemen outside our street, we should be safe.'

'I have no objection,' the AC said. 'I can send two men today. But you'll become branded in the eyes of the people for no reason and might even give the impression that you're asking for trouble. Anyway, on Friday at whatever time you feel the need, just give me a call and I'll send as many armed policemen as you want.'

By the time Bashir Ahmad reached Ismail's store he heard the call for the Asr prayer coming from the mosque's loudspeaker. Greetings over, Bashir Ahmad said laughing, 'Much as I'd like to enjoy your company for a bit, observing prayers on time is also necessary, for such is God's command. An Ahmadi offering prayer in the presence of a Muslim is a cognizable offence in the national law. There are so many conflicting religious and legal demands on me. Now, you tell me what I should do.'

Ismail laughed as he took out the prayer rug from the cupboard. 'Chaudhry sahib, just say your prayers. This talk can wait.'

'So you are bent on being an accessory to the crime! I'm warning you: you can be punished for it as much as I.'

'No problem. I'm fed up anyway staying outside for so long. I wouldn't mind an opportunity for a change of air for a few days. I hear life inside a prison is quite unusual. If nothing else, I may be able to see that new world thanks to you. Should I tell you one thing, Chaudhry sahib?'

'Sure.'

'No Muslim has ever had a chance to say his prayers on this mat. I have put it aside only for non-Muslims, both the current ones and those who will become so in the future. You say your prayers on it, or sometimes Hasnain Shah, if he happens to be around. One of you has already been declared a non-Muslim; demands for the other to be declared a non-Muslim are in the works. The incidents of murder as punishment are besides those demands.'

As Bashir Ahmad got busy with performing his prayers, Ismail's mind wandered off to the cataclysmic days of Partition. Whole populations were migrating across the border in the midst of unrelenting slaughter, leaving him utterly depressed about his own distress and that of others. Yet there was something that had sustained him and given his sagging spirit a boost. 'It will be different in Pakistan, in a country created only for the followers of Islam; at least we'll find enduring relief from the Hindu–Muslim strife that has poisoned our daily life in united India.' But what a shame! In spite of such heavy sacrifices, the old evil had resurrected itself, this time in a ghastlier form. Perhaps there is some inherent depravity in man's nature that repeatedly forces him, for one reason or another, to soak his hands in human blood. Ismail couldn't understand why this was so.

A large-hearted person who offended neither himself nor others, Ismail's favourite and most pleasurable pastime was to get together and gossip with his friends, who included men of every faith and school of thought. He welcomed them at his store and showed them hospitality to the extent he could. He was a thinking man and fond of reading. He had an opinion on every important issue. He did express his views, but without ever wanting to impose them on anyone, nor did he want others to impose theirs on him. One idea that he stuck by steadfastly was that suffering and comfort, especially on account of wealth or women, were entirely one's private matters and it was unbecoming to talk about them. He wasn't fated to receive any comfort from a woman or wealth, but he never shared his unhappiness with anyone. When with friends, he laughed and made others laugh; alone, at night, he would cry as if he were looking at the familiar face of his old sufferings for the first time. During the fury of Partition, his parents, brothers, sisters and all his other relatives were put to death for the crime of being Muslims. Cheerful and happy Barkatay, the fountain of a fragrant warbling life for him, escaped being murdered in the mass slaughter only to be abducted by her assailants. He found that out one morning in the newspaper when he saw her name in the list of women recovered from East Punjab. That Barkatay was alive and in Pakistan made his heart swell with such joy that he thought it would burst through its walls. Inebriated with excitement, he left for Lahore the same instant, as though he were returning to the Gobindpur of three years ago where nothing had changed, and everything and everyone was the same as he had seen them since his childhood. Over and over he tried to persuade himself that it was only the ravaged Barkatay Bibi whom the army had recovered and brought to Lahore; it hadn't picked up and brought over all the residents of the Gobindpur of three years ago, but he had little success. Logic and understanding aren't the only things needed to live! In some matters a person must also allow himself to be deceived wittingly. After running around for three or four days, when he finally encountered Barkatay Bibi, a woman once so proud of her allure and beauty, what he saw before him was a hesitant, cold and broken woman. Who was she? He stood aghast. Nothing of the old Barkatay remained. In her empty, barren eyes, there wasn't even a shred of her old confidence. All the vanity of that proud woman had been dashed to the ground. The infinite sadness in her face was so profuse it seemed to fill the entire room. What had India's freedom done to her?

'My God! What's happened, Barkatay?'

'Wish I knew. I've been tossed about like a battered fallen leaf.' She broke into tears.

'Have some courage, Barkatay.'

'Courage for what? Nothing's been spared. There's only a life that neither ends nor continues. It's just stuck in my chest.'

'Why do you despair so much? There will be better days.'

'Ismail, a day that is gone never returns. There's night

before the next day. How am I going to live through the night?'

'Barkatay, you have no one left in the world, and neither do I. You can't stay in the camp your whole life, can you? Come with me. No one from our village has reached Pakistan. Who else can you stay with?'

Quickly she agreed to go with him. He brought the apparition of the Barkatay of Gobindpur with him to Sultanpur. He tried very hard to restore Barkatay to her former self, but it was impossible. When he proposed marriage, tears welled up in her eyes, but she showed her consent with a nod of her head. Her soul had melted away, only her body was still there, working like a clock, without a will of its own. A year and a half later a boy was born to them. At her insistence, they named him Ramzan, after her son who had been killed in Gobindpur. Ismail saw some cheerfulness return to her face after Ramzan's birth, but only for a while. Then she fell sick and six months later she passed away, followed a few months later by the infant's death. Ismail was convinced that the boy died because of his mother's absence, while it was India's freedom that had killed the mother.

Many times Ismail asked her about the attack and what transpired in its aftermath, but her only response was that she couldn't recall anything. One Sunday morning, she was sitting in the courtyard feeding baby Ramzan in her lap, smiling and talking to him: 'My son will grow up and be as brave as a lion; he'll never give ground, no matter how badly the earth shakes as the kingdoms change.'

Ismail sat opposite her on the cot reading his newspaper. Suddenly, remembering something he'd forgotten, he said:

'Barkatay, you haven't said a word about the attack on Gobindpur. Can't you recall anything?'

'Yes, I remember this much: when you left, the whole mohalla seemed as if it had lost its sense of pride and sunk into unmitigated despair. Taja shook his head and said that they had lost half the battle even before it began. He didn't realize he'd lost all of it. Within a few days after you left, the isolated Muslim families from the neighbouring villages began scrambling over to our mohalla for shelter. Before long, quite a large number had gathered. Your folks didn't stir from their house in the city, nor did they inquire about us. Then all means of communication were cut off: we couldn't even find out anything about them. We did everything we could to look after the families that had come to our place. There were so many that every piece of flat ground, the roofs, courtyards, rooms and storerooms were all packed with people. In our house alone there were nearly thirty women and children. Taja distributed the swords, lances and axes that you had purchased among the thirty or forty young men, and posted them to guard our house and everywhere else around the mohalla, including the street's entrance and exit, and he kept walking around the whole night. During the day, Baba Shahu instructed the young men in the use of the weapons, as much as he himself knew. Five or six shots were fired one night as we slept. Everyone woke up scared. It must have been around midnight. Suddenly a noise rose from the direction of the mosque. Baba Shahu came running along the street shouting, "Watch out, there's been an attack!" Sounds of crying and lamentation shot up from every house. Ten or twelve Sikhs, brandishing their kirpans, barged into our house and started butchering women and children. Two Sikh soldiers with proper guns accompanied them. One of them screamed, "Don't spare anyone!" The right and the wrong in this world will only be sorted out in the next. It seems to me that every killer is right and every victim is wrong. The fire and high flames in the mosque and the houses around it produced so much light you could even see a needle. Ramzan was sleeping with me but I have no idea when, in that panic and tumult, he got up and walked away somewhere. I never saw him again. Perhaps he went looking for his father. I was shouting for Taja, who was on guard duty. When one Sikh raised his sword to kill me, another said, "Oh no, don't. She's worth keeping," and moved forward and grabbed my arm . . .'

'Enough Barkatay, enough! Please stop!' Ismail yelled as he cried, overcome by emotion.

'You're the one who ran away, abandoning Gobindpur to its fate. You must listen to the whole story. Didn't you keep asking every day: How were my parents killed? What happened to my brothers and sisters? Who came? When? How many? Was there anyone from Gobindpur among them?—as if people trapped in such confusion can think or reason. You should have stayed and watched. Everything was over within two minutes and then there was nothing but dreadful silence. A person who is killed or is spared knows only one story—the one he's been through.'

Lying face down on the cot, Ismail's body writhed with sobs that would not let up. Barkatay picked up the child sleeping on the cot and went inside. Her stinging jibe made him feel as if, in the youthful throbbing moonlight, he was standing horrified and alone in the middle of a graveyard, and everywhere, as far as his eyes could see, there was nothing but graves, with neither a tree nor a building anywhere in sight. A dark heart-rending scream rose from somewhere, passed through the middle of his body, pierced the moonlight, and flew up towards the moon. He watched it for some time and then it vanished.

While Bashir Ahmad was saying his prayers, Shaikh Sardar Ali, Sufi Ghafoor and Haji Manzoor arrived—they all had their stores in the same big bazaar and were daily visitors. By the time Bashir Ahmad finished telling his beads and was folding the prayer mat, Noor Muhammad Chauhan and Chaudhry Muhammad Ali also walked in. Chauhan used to publish a weekly paper from Sultanpur that carried only local news.

The paper was just an excuse to eulogize and shower accolades on officials posted in Sultanpur, or those among the local gentry who, after a nod from the officials, presented Chauhan with gifts and offerings. People wishing to have the details of their so-called social activities published in his weekly would have them printed, in bold or regular fonts, in a large space or small, in accordance with the fees they could afford. At one time Chauhan was an ardent supporter of communism and he still believed the cure for the ills of Pakistan and other backward countries lay in adopting a socialist system. But all his revolutionary talk was reserved for social conversations; there was no place for it in his own newspaper. He was not above bending over backwards to secure an objective. When, at times, in order to achieve his objective, he needed to put out his hand to beg, he did that without hesitation. He believed that every profession had its particular difficulties, and a professional had to accept them, whether he liked it or not. His academic education was next to nil, but with hard work and study, he had acquired considerable facility with words and had a deep understanding of current affairs. In his conversations he was as sharp as a naked sword, but nonetheless a sword fashioned from cardboard, given the servile and ingratiating nature of his newspaper. He was usually hard up, making ends meet with difficulty, and so addicted to talking that whenever he got an opportunity he just sat and let torrents of eloquence flow without pause for hours. At such times absolutely nothing mattered: his financial difficulties, his wife, children, important business—everything was washed from his mind.

Chaudhry Muhammad Ali was a small landholder of unassuming attire. He'd graduated during the time of the British and looked hard for a government job but didn't find one. Disappointed, he sought refuge in his ancestral profession of landholding and found it. He was content with his circumstances. It had been fifty years since his graduation, and even though the degree had proved useless, if anyone even now, verbally or in writing, added the letters BA to his name, he felt intoxicated with pride. He came to visit Ismail now and then from his village to talk about the new developments in contemporary affairs.

Placing the prayer mat in the cupboard, Bashir Ahmad asked, 'What were you saying, Uncle Ismail?'

'Just that finally sectarianism has sprouted in Pakistan. Innocent people are being mercilessly put to death every other day.'

'At the time the Punjab was being partitioned, whether or not any area joined Pakistan depended on the number of Muslims in that area,' observed Bashir Ahmad. 'That was the important criterion in those days. In those days we were lovingly being included among the Muslims. The person whose efforts brought Pakistan into being was a Shiʿa, but no one objected. People unanimously accepted him as the Quaid-e-Azam. Now the maulvis are calling Shiʿas infidels and getting them killed. We Ahmadis have already been declared non-Muslims, now it's the Shiʿas' turn. Common folk are still as unconcerned as they were when the movement against us started. The government is doing nothing to suppress this movement, nor is it taking any steps to guarantee our safety.'

Hearing Bashir's objection, Haji Manzoor probed his brains hard but found no answer. In embarrassment he started scratching his beard and looking towards Shaikh Sardar Ali in the hope of hearing an appropriate rejoinder. Before Partition, Haji Manzoor used to sell vegetables on a pushcart in a village of eastern Punjab. When he came to Sultanpur, a cloth merchant's store which was full of fabric worth thousands of rupees was allotted to him; thus, in the space of one day, a pauper became a prince, which he considered a special providential favour to him. Despite his knowledge of the essence of religion, he regarded fasting and praying only as a means to augment his wealth, a sort of substitute for Aladdin's magic. But he never could persuade himself to part with money, even if it was in compliance with the religious duty to pay *zakat*. His previous experience, even though acquired in a minor trade, came in very handy in his new profession. With his dedication and hard work he became a successful businessman. He was an active worker in the Ahrar Party before Partition; after it, even though he lost faith in his old allegiance, his prejudice against the Ahmadis persevered. To save his skin, when he was obliged to seek shelter in Pakistan, previously the object of his scorn, he shed whatever little pride he had left. He forsook practical politics and threw himself headlong into the textile business. Now he was a prosperous man. 'Bashir sahib, please don't make false allegations,' Shaikh Sardar Ali remarked. 'It was your people who started sectarian discord in 1948 when Chaudhry Zafarullah Khan refused to offer Jinnah sahib's funeral prayer and stood apart from a crowd of a hundred thousand and just watched them perform it.'

Haji Manzoor laughed at Sardar Ali's comment and chirped, 'Touché! Answer that one.'

Bashir replied, 'It was wrong of Chaudhry sahib to just watch Jinnah sahib's funeral prayer, but to punish a whole community for one individual's mistake and go on punishing it continually for forty years, believing all along it hadn't been punished enough, well, this is hardly a proper attitude, is it?'

'No, Bashir sahib, the exact opposite is true,' Sardar Ali shot back. 'From the day Ahmadiyyat was launched, your community has sought nothing other than to establish its distinct and unique identity, to be distinguished from the rest of the Muslims. Isn't that why you people have strictly forbidden your followers to perform funeral prayers for the dead of other faiths? This is how you safeguard your community from merging into the larger Muslim nation. Of course you had a right to do that, but please don't say that Zafarullah Khan erred in avoiding Jinnah sahib's funeral prayer. He was only following the orders of the organization. So if now the majority Muslims have separated themselves from you, to set themselves apart from the Ahmadis, you should be happy that they have fulfilled your own desire and legalized it.'

'Well, all right, let it be so,' Bashir Ahmad observed.

'But surely it is not so unusual for two members of a single community not to wish to promote too much interaction between them and keep their social contacts to a minimum. Do you think they don't have the right to do so? Would it result in excommunication from their community? According to Islam, if I attest with my heart that I'm a Muslim and proclaim it with my tongue, then I'm a Muslim in every sense of the word. But a law made by men tells me that, no, I am not a Muslim. When Islam has already entrusted me with the right to decide who I might be, why is this man-made law interfering in my affairs?'

Chauhan interrupted, 'It's futile now to argue who is a Muslim and who is not. The Quaid-e-Azam had already settled the issue in his address of 11 August 1947, when he claimed that all citizens of Pakistan would be equal regardless of their differences. Now it's another matter that some people suppressed this address because it didn't fit in with their own interest. This statement can only mean one thing: all citizens will have the same rights and responsibilities, and religious affiliation would be a personal matter, which the state would not interfere in. It will not be possible much longer to hide the Quaid's address and the guiding principles enshrined in it for framing government policy. I think it is necessary for me now to write an exhaustive article on this issue and publish it in my newspaper.'

That made everyone laugh in their hearts for they knew all too well that Chauhan would never attempt to write and publish an article on such a controversial issue. Bashir Ahmad said, 'And yet, quite against Jinnah's dictates we were declared non-Muslims and the declaration was made part of the Constitution. All right, fine, but if you can't treat us as Muslims at least treat us as humans. Why, we're not even given the status of animals, let alone humans. Even animals are accorded feelings and emotions to some extent, but we . . . no more than rocks. The townsfolk are forced to swear at our venerable moral preceptors and teachers by name. The speech-mongers get on the stage and incite ordinary people against us so they storm our houses, plunder them, and then set them on fire and kill everyone inside. No one is ever caught. We can't say our prayers, give the *azan*, or refer to our mosque as a mosque. What's all this? The townsfolk see this cruelty taking place, yet say nothing.'

Chauhan said, 'Chaudhry sahib, there's no reason to become emotional. When cruelty goes beyond a certain limit, it generates its own reaction from within itself.'

'You don't mean to say—do you—that, God forbid, Islam would disappear from this country?' Haji Manzoor said in a huff. 'Pakistan has no meaning besides "There is no God but One." This was the slogan that was heard echoing from every street in the heyday of the Pakistan Movement. I saw all this with my own eyes, and that was what helped us succeed. If you go back on your word to God, His punishment will surely descend on you.'

Chauhan answered, 'To begin with, this slogan didn't exist in those days, at least it had nothing to do with the Muslim League. And even if we suppose that it did exist, no one can explain what it really meant or what its purpose was. The most that can be said is that Pakistan was created for those who recited the kalima. If that is so, on what grounds were Ahmadis excluded from the faith? They too recite the kalima, don't they? How did you assume from this slogan that Pakistan was created only for the Sunnis to do what they will? Haji-ji, you need to unite all Pakistanis, regardless of their religious beliefs. Forget about differences; this is the only way to save the country. How long will you go on dividing the country on the basis of language, nationality, caste, family, religion and sect? How many will you declare as infidels? You'll end up splintering the country that way. Have you already forgotten how East Pakistan broke away? It all started with language, remember? God will not punish unity, but disunity He surely will. People are hemmed in by a plethora of problems; solve those first. Don't worry about who is or isn't a Muslim; those are all secondary issues. How long will you go on embroiling people in complications unrelated to their problems and lead them astray?'

'If all you wanted was to create an irreligious state, why did you have to go through the trouble of Partition and the loss of so many lives?' Sardar Ali piped in.

Chauhan responded, 'Providence had given us a single leader of sound thinking and extraordinary political discernment, and he wanted Pakistan not to be a religious state. Later on, some people, out of sheer perversity, threw this notion overboard; hence the animosity and chaos you are witnessing in public life today. By the way, Shaikh sahib, you were one of Pakistan's detractors when it came into being, weren't you? By what right do you now try to claim what its character should be?'

Sardar Ali was distressed by this and responded, 'After all, you're a communist, an enemy of God and His Prophet. What would you know of the greatness of Islam? Why, you were tooting your Russian horn all the time! Don't you see what became of Russia? Got blown to pieces!'

Ismail warned in an imperious tone, 'If you're going to

get personal, I'll end this session. Is this any way to talk?' That silenced everyone.

As a young man, Sufi Ghafoor had walked all the way to Pakistan, with his family in a caravan, from his native Haryana. There, after completing vernacular middle school, he had started working with his father as a weaver. When they came over to Sultanpur, his father was allotted a utensils store, so he began selling pots and pans, and was still plying the same trade. For the first time in his life he experienced prosperity in Pakistan, which had made him even more humble. He always wore a white turban of unstarched coarse muslin, which now seemed whiter than before, and sported a longish salt-and-pepper beard. In assemblies such as the one at Ismail's, he would sit, his hands folded on his stomach, as if performing his ritual prayers, his eyes cast down, and listen quietly and attentively to every word that was spoken. He said, 'There's such a dearth of love in the world that if I could buy it in exchange for my life, I would distribute it among the starving populace. We should give people the sweetness of love; it costs nothing. We shouldn't inject the bitterness of dread and panic into their lives. As it is, we've embittered life quite enough already. Let people follow whatever path they desire. Ultimately, every path, however circuitous, leads to the door of the same Creator. There isn't any other door it might wander off to. All claims and jeers are the work of the devilish ego. To quietly arouse vanity, consider others contemptible, and teach a person to be conceited—these are all among its wiles and tactics. We get trapped in its net very easily, but find it hard to escape. We should instead try to create ease and comfort for others; if we can't do that, we should at least refrain from adding to their difficulties.'

Haji Manzoor said, 'Without a doubt, that Sufi has spoken some very sweet words, but let me tell you one thing: the Ahmadis are so narrow-minded and prejudiced that if they were in as big a majority today as other Muslims, they would have made it impossible for us to even breathe normally or save our skins. Compared to what they would have done to us, we are hardly doing anything to them.'

Everyone spontaneously burst out laughing. Ismail said, 'Haji-ji, one has to admit that Sufi's words have made a very good impression on you.'

'Haji sahib's comment was blown out of proportion,' Sardar Ali interjected after the laughing died down. 'All right, it was untimely. But if you think about it, it bears being considered seriously and carries a lot of weight.'

Chaudhry Muhammad Ali quickly remarked, 'If suppositions are what you base your discussion of these issues on, you'll wander far from the truth. Keep today's situation in mind when you talk.'

Just then Munir Ahmad arrived at the entrance to Ismail's store and offered his greetings. They all became quiet. Everybody knew that Bashir and Munir were closely related. Everyone gaped at Munir wondering what news had sent him hither looking for Bashir. A tingling sensation suddenly ran down Bashir's spine, as though his legs had become lifeless. Fearfully, he asked, 'Is everything all right, Munir?'

'Yes, it is. Don't be worried. I just came to ask for permission to return to Noor Nagar. If you need me again, I can come back tomorrow.'

'You're starting so late. It's going to get dark before you get there. You know the situation we're in these days. Wouldn't it be better if you left tomorrow?'

'I've got to be there tonight. Many things need to be taken care of. There are three or four of us together. Nothing to worry about.'

'All right. May God keep you safe! Don't bother coming back tomorrow. We'll call you when we need you.'

After Munir's departure, the gathering resumed its prior character and Chauhan began talking. 'Three people—Sir Sayyid Ahmad Khan, Allama Iqbal and the Quaid-e-Azam—were the benefactors of this nation, and yet every one of them had the verdict of *kufr* cast against him in his time. The reactionary forces, however, were never as powerful in their day and age as they are today. Usurper heads of state and untrustworthy and inefficient political leaders have, for their selfish purposes, blown so much air into this beast called reaction that it has swelled all out of proportion, while in truth people have been repeatedly rejecting these same reactionary forces for the past one hundred and fifty years. If this weren't the case, none of these three benefactors would ever have succeeded. The common folk want to walk in step with the times, while these reactionary forces wrapping themselves around their skirts drag them backwards.'

Bashir Ahmad said, 'I agree that the Muslim people have sided with new demands at every important turning point in the national life. Now listen, we managed to disregard the harassment mounted against us by some reactionaries at the behest of one politician in 1953 as a bad dream. But since 1974, Ahmadis have been subjected to a whole series of incidents of various kinds of terror, which are still continuing. Every national government has participated verbally, financially, as well as practically. Inhuman laws were instituted under which fraudulent court cases were filed against us, and to this day there is no end in sight. The majority group is totally indifferent to our plight. Even though they're not with the reactionaries, they allow themselves to be incited and used by them. There is another relationship besides Islam, it's humanity, and people all over the world stand up in support of the victim and against tyranny, sometimes even risking their lives. But here, well, no one bats an eyelid. Everyone knows the miserable life of the Ahmadis, yet everyone remains silent and totally uninvolved. Perhaps their hearts have turned to stone, or maybe their minds have lost the ability to comprehend.'

Chauhan objected, 'Bashir sahib, you're wrong to think that ordinary folks are unconcerned or hard-hearted. On an individual level, many people are sympathetic to Ahmadis. You can see it easily from the people gathered here. But common people are no better than a crowd. And until some leader shows it the way and determines its direction, a crowd is like a flock of animals wandering in the darkness. Unfortunately, the right and proper leadership has been missing from our politics; what little leadership there is, is used to affect people's feelings for the leaders' own political interests. The reactionary circles would never have succeeded in creating such a big rift between the Muslims and the Ahmadis if your community itself hadn't been party to it. The Ahmadi jamaʿat is a strong, organized, well-knit group with vast resources, as all exemplary organizations should be, but it has never tried to come to grips with the problems of ordinary Muslims, nor has it lighted their way towards progress. It has exerted all its energies towards keeping itself separate from ordinary Muslims. Perhaps it was a question of identity for you people, but shouldn't you perhaps have kept it within moderate limits? You drove people away and they went. Then again, of all the traditional and reactionary religious organizations, yours is the most shackled by tradition and reaction. All you've ever done is proselytize, but have you ever joined with ordinary Muslims on any common social, humanitarian, literary or cultural platform to develop contacts with them? So, all the other conservative, reactionary bodies like your own started butting heads with you. What else did you expect? If all your missionary work yielded one convert out of a thousand, what else could the remaining nine hundred and ninety-nine feel but that they were the prey and you were the hunters. And when did you ever hear a hunter worrying his head over the problems of the prey? All he wants is to hunt down the prey and bag it. At first people got annoyed and then disgusted with this behaviour. With all your devotion to Quaid-e-Azam, did it ever occur to you to build a hospital in his name where everyone, irrespective of faith or belief, could receive treatment? You could have built a university for higher studies in science in an undeveloped country.'

Sardar Ali saw an opportunity to butt in. 'The organizers of the Ahmadiyyah jamaʿat have the mentality of the banias, petty moneylenders,' he observed with a tinge of sarcasm. 'What do they care about any country, nation, people, or even their own religion, which they view as yet another means of making money? They're only interested in gathering as many sheep into their fold as possible and getting as much wool out of them as they can to swell their coffers. They only have one slogan: Make Ahmadis and more Ahmadis so the money keeps coming.'

'Look, friends, it's not our way to poke fun at someone's

belief,' Ismail interjected, 'so that it hurts him. We get together to understand each other's point of view, don't we? And we do that to strengthen love among us, not to spread hatred. If you can't change the way you speak, better try not to show up here again.'

Sardar Ali felt he needed to explain his position. 'I was only talking about the attitude of the jamaʿat; I wasn't trying to hurt the feelings of anyone,' he said.

Ismail said, 'Look, you just repeated what Chauhan sahib was saying, only more derisively. It might have cooled your anger; it certainly didn't help anyone else.'

'If my comments have hurt Bashir sahib or anyone else, I apologize.'

Bashir said, 'It's nothing. We're used to objections in whatever tone or accent they're hurled at us. The good Lord knows well whether our missionary work is for collecting money or for spreading our faith to the four corners of the world. We're answerable to Him alone. Regarding Chauhan sahib's comments, I'll say this on the basis of what I know of our jamaʿat's thinking. The jamaʿat would have faced objections every step of the way had it built a hospital or university, and in the end those institutions would have become victims of terror and might even have unwittingly become an additional source of clashes . . .'

'Bashir sahib,' Chauhan interrupted, 'it wasn't an objection, only a suggestion. If you look carefully, Muslims have the same sort of objection to Ismailis as they do to the Ahmadis. But this hasn't stopped the Ismailis from setting up a medical university and a hospital of international calibre in Karachi. Did anyone object or throw a monkey wrench? No, none. Not then, and not now. In the far-flung northern regions of the country, the Ismailis have established a considerable number of small hospitals, schools and water-delivery schemes. True, there's a sizeable population of Ismailis in these areas, but a fraternal atmosphere has been created there between the Ismailis and non-Ismailis so that an environment of tolerance for Ismaili beliefs has come into being.'

Muhammad Ali chuckled and addressed Chauhan. 'Chauhan sahib, understand one thing: civility is not a right, nor does a person demand it. I notice that you're probably asking the Ahmadi jamaʿat to present Islam in a modernized form like the Ismailis, while, in fact, Ahmadis are every bit as traditional and conservative as all the other religious groups, and are equally inclined towards the past. Ahmadis only differ from other groups in one aspect of belief; as for the rest, like all fundamentalists, Ahmadis think that the bulk of human problems and difficulties disappear as soon as one has verbally uttered the kalima. And if they don't disappear, then surely it's the result of some blemish in the quality of the faith of the person who utters the kalima; hence their overly zealous insistence on missionary work. Now you're influenced by socialism. And socialism regards this world as the only reality and demands every kind of social and economic justice right here and now. So, as I understand it, human compassion is the only realm in which you two can come together. You can and should oppose oppression in this realm. As a Muslim, I also condemn every kind of inequity and oppression.'

Chauhan answered, 'Muhammad Ali sahib, what you say is correct. I am quite familiar with the beliefs and conduct of the Ahmadis, and I'm not trying to persuade them to modernize themselves. All I want is for this tension that exists between them and the majority to end somehow, so Ahmadis will be able to maintain their beliefs and live their lives without fear. I've used the example of the Ismailis simply because such a thing can happen. Surely, other people and Ahmadis are quite capable of thinking up better ways to begin tolerating each other's point of view, but more than any other group, I think the Ahmadis need to initiate the move.'

Just then some young students from the theological seminary were passing by on board a crawling tonga, making announcements over a loudspeaker about the rally the day after. The rally was spearheaded by the 'Seal of Prophethood Conference' people and was scheduled to take place after the Juma congregational prayer. The rally was going to expose the Ahmadis' collusion with Hindus and Jews, and details of the Ahmadi conspiracy against Pakistan and the Muslim world. It was to be addressed by Pakistan's well-known scholars, speakers and orators who would expose the false claims about prophethood made by the Qadianis.

'Folks, you heard that, didn't you?—perhaps a foretaste of what's to come at the rally,' Bashir Ahmad lamented. 'Now why wouldn't such accusations infuriate people? We repeatedly told the officials that the conference being held under their auspices will have nothing but venomous propaganda against us and that the audience, driven mad by grief and anger, will come after us, but would they listen? They kept saying the same thing: we won't let them do it. Who can dare ask them now? If we also were allowed to speak in our defence at the rally and the audience were to hear us out, we would prove that we're not a threat at all to the people's faith, or the Islamic world or even Pakistan. If there is a threat, it is to the illegal economic and material interests of certain individuals—the real movers and promoters of this conference.'

'All of us have been witness, in one form or another, to the ghastly face of the riots of 1947,' Ismail remarked with an undertone of commiseration. 'Bashir Ahmad was perhaps too young to have retained any memory of those dreadful days. But at least four of us were grown up when we escaped East Punjab and made it to Pakistan. How we feared for our lives! Surely, you must have experienced the horror of death hovering over your heads, at least for a few days if not for longer.'

'Brother Ismail,' Sufi Ghafoor joined in and said, 'our caravan reached Pakistan by the Ganda Singh Wala route after four months of walking on foot and travelling by ox-carts. I'll never forget that doomsday torment we endured every single minute of that awful flight. We spent our nights in mortal fear of being attacked any minute and the severity of our perilous trek kept us on edge all through the day. Children, women with newborn babies, and old men began dying in droves. Whenever the caravan decamped after resting somewhere, it left a long trail of graves behind it along the side of the road. As soon as we crossed the boundary of Pakistan my heart swelled and cried out: Please, God, don't ever let us go through that kind of ordeal again!'

Ismail added to Sufi Ghafoor's comment, 'In those days fear swirled in the pit of our stomachs and never left us; day and night, it kept gnawing at us bit by bit. We were so listless that nothing interested us. And despair drove us to want to die. It seemed a lot easier to die fighting instead of being hurled into a state of lethal suspense. Those who have been through such torment ought really to stop and think about how Ahmadis have been suspended between life and death for years, strung on the same crucifix of uncertainty.'

'At least you had a tangible refuge in the shape of Pakistan that you could look forward to,' Bashir Ahmad interjected. 'But what have we got—not even the blurry traces of a destination that might give our sagging spirits a boost.'

They all fell quiet for some time, as though their consciences were calling them to account. Then Sufi cleared his throat, broke the silence and said, 'No religion allows anyone to be high-handed or cruel in its name. In the matter of faith particularly, Islam has forbidden the use of coercion. Everyone is allowed to do as he pleases, even accept a stone as a god. No one else need be troubled by it. In our egomania, let's not stretch our truth so much that it makes life unbearable for others. When cruelty reaches its limit, God's wrath comes into play. Beware of that time, for nothing will be spared after that.'

'Not just the Ahmadis, the Shiʿas, Sikhs, Christians, Parsees, Hindus—everyone except the Sunni majority feels insecure in Pakistan,' Chauhan observed. 'Those among them who have the means and the opportunity are fleeing the country. This state of affairs creates doubts about the survival of Pakistan, but the government is doing nothing about it. The public is a dumb majority and becomes even dumber in the face of organized groups. The maulvis and students of the theological schools are a relatively small body, but they're well organized and vocal. They demonstrate their power in the streets and ultimately force the government to retreat on every front. God knows what sensitive information they have that they can bend the government like this.'

'Chauhan sahib, even among the Sunnis there are many

sects which don't get along,' Sufi remarked. 'When everybody else is smashed, they'll start destroying each other. You can't limit that.'

'You're absolutely right,' Chauhan affirmed. 'To save the country from internal disintegration and create national unity, it would be better to return to the policy laid out by the Quaid-e-Azam in his 11 August speech, a policy for the exact situation in the country. It would be good to resurrect and enforce it, in whatever way possible. He was a sagacious, discerning and competent political leader and he had prescribed that policy after carefully evaluating the temperament of the people.'

It was quiet in the street when Bashir Ahmad returned. The kids, tired from playing in the street all evening, had gone home. He saw the light from his office cast a square shadow of the grillework on to the darkened surface of the street as it came filtering through the window, and the whispering buzz of his waiting clients conveyed to him their fly-like pointless unease, which he knew would cease as soon as he entered the office. Seeing him, the white spot of light enclosed by the darkness around it chirped naturally like a bird trapped in its cage, its twittering meant only for his ears. He liked it. He looked at it again, but this time it remained quiet. The door opening into the courtyard of the house was bolted from the inside today. He knocked. His wife came to the door and asked, 'Who is it?'

'It's me.'

As she undid the latch she said, 'You took so long getting home. I felt as if my life was in the balance the whole time. You know very well what a terrible time we're going through these days. Master Lateef and Brother Anwaar arrived home long ago. Where did you disappear to?'

'Didn't they tell you? I went to the bazaar for a while. To visit Uncle Ismail.'

'What did the officials say?'

'Nothing much. They just kept encouraging us. The town is as quiet as ever. I just had a look. There hasn't been any activity. Except that there were some lads from the religious school going around in a tonga announcing the upcoming rally.'

'God willing, the day of the rally will also pass without problems.' Then, as if reassuring herself, she said, 'Let come what may. It's pointless to get ourselves worked up.'

'We did all we could. Tomorrow we'll see what happens. Anyway, we don't have a choice.'

'I have a suggestion.'

'Yes, what?'

'Shouldn't we pack our valuables and your books and send them to Noor Nagar tomorrow on an ox-cart?'

'No, we can't do that. It will create panic in the whole street. The unity we need for collective protection will disappear and there'll be an individual stampede to safety. Anyone who might otherwise be disinclined may take advantage of such circumstances to attack. Where's Mubashshir?'

'Nasira came asking if the official had given any answer. She waited for a long time. When you didn't show up, she left and took Mubashshir along. She said he'd been feeling scared since yesterday. Didn't even go out in the street in the evening to play. Talking might help dispel his fear and some of my own frightening thoughts.'

'Did you meet with any of the neighbours?'

'Yes. In the morning I first went to visit Taj Bibi. I thought if she could let go of her former resentment and come over here, why couldn't I go see her? Even though I knew it was fear that had brought her here, I went to visit her anyway.'

'That was nice of you. When one is beset by difficulties, it's better to let go of petty gripes. What did she say?'

'What else could she say? Just cried her heart out. Her house is chock-full of the dowry stuff for her two daughters. If rioting gets under way, she fears everything will be destroyed. How will she get the girls wed if that happens?'

'God will be merciful.'

'After I sat down, Master Lateef's daughter-in-law Kulsum, Phuphi Zainab, Nasira's sister-in-law Fatima, Batool, Qudsia and Lord knows how many others also came in.'

'Yeah? So what did you talk about?'

'Is there any other subject anywhere these days besides "What's going to happen?" The same question echoes everywhere. Had there been only one household, its inmates would have gone crazy from fear. Since there are many, we take heart from seeing each other, and pray to God, singly and collectively, for our safety.'

'Did Masi Jannat show up too? She's quite chummy-chummy with Taj Bibi, isn't she?'

Amtul started to laugh and said, 'She got held up today. She took our advice. To stop Munawwar from wandering around the city, she locked him up inside. She can't very well move around herself, can she? So she's sitting by the window outside consoling him. In the morning he was very angry. We could hear his screams even here. He's quieter now, but Masi hasn't let him go. She still has him locked up.'

Early in the morning, as Bashir Ahmad slept in the courtyard under the open sky, he didn't wake up slowly as was normal. His eyes popped open suddenly, as if someone had hit the light switch. The first thought that shot through his mind was that Friday had finally come. What did God have in store for them that day? May the good Lord be merciful! The sounds of the azan came rippling through the air from loudspeakers everywhere. The night had been oppressively sultry, but a pleasant breeze was blowing now. Fresh, glistening, white jasmine was scattering its heady fragrance everywhere in the courtyard. A swelled-up jujube tree stood out front, making a noise like a clucking hen. Deep inside the tree, a tiny sparrow on a branch made a short peep to check whether morning had come yet, just as Bashir Ahmad had thought that perhaps that day wasn't Friday when he first opened his eyes. On the adjoining cot, Amtul slept soundly with her hand on Mubashshir. Shaking her, Bashir said, 'Get up now. You'll miss the Fajr prayer.' In this house too, the everyday routine soon took over the newborn day. Bashir Ahmad got ready to go to the courts. Placing his breakfast before him, his wife said, 'It would be better if you didn't go to the courts today. Who knows what might happen.'

'Nothing will happen. There's no need to get nervous. My clients will be lined up outside the courts, waiting impatiently. If I don't show up on time, I'll be derelict in my duty. And look, the courts are the nerve centre of the district. News of all sorts of incidents reaches there first. Appropriate steps can be taken expeditiously if you learn early enough about any change in the situation. Sitting at home there's little I can do to ensure the safety of a handful of Ahmadis in Sultanpur. Seriously, you don't think our house is a sanctuary, do you? It isn't for us, anyway. For the others we're like fish in water-pots. They'll grab us and throw us whenever they want, and we'll be dead and gone. In the event of an attack, we would be killed like flies with a spray pump if we're inside. Our safety lies in only one thing: that riots don't start at all. We can't just stop them cooped up inside the house.'

Amtul heard him but didn't say anything and started crying, so bitterly that her body convulsed with the silent intensity of her sobs. Bashir Ahmad gathered her in his arms, kissed her on the forehead and said, 'You have to give courage to the other women. How will you do that if you lose heart yourself? In hard times, if a person forgoes patience and endurance, wouldn't that be like admitting defeat even before the battle has begun?'

'It's all right. You go now. I'm okay. I was overcome momentarily. It's over now. I have complete trust in God that He will protect us.'

'The rally will be held after the Juma prayer. I and the other workers from the street will be home after the prayer.'

As Bashir Ahmad came out he saw three policemen standing outside the street's iron gate. One of them even had a Kalashnikov with him. They recognized Bashir Ahmad, greeted him, informed him that the officials had sent them there to safeguard the street and had asked them to let him know about it. Bashir Ahmad said, 'Thank you and your officers very much. But your presence here at this time is unnecessary; it may even be provocative. It would be better if you came here after the Juma prayer. Please let your officers know that three people may not be enough if riots break out. It would be more effective if your number could be increased to ten.' After he left, the policemen consulted among themselves for some time and then walked back to the police station.

Bashir Ahmad finished his work at the court around half past twelve. As he was getting ready to go home, he heard an unsubstantiated report that some burned sheets of the Qurʾan were found in Noor Nagar. No details were available about where those sheets had come from, under what circumstances they were discovered, or who was responsible for burning them. He immediately sensed that surely this devilry was pre-planned to implicate the Ahmadis. Anyone could have guessed that on that day of all days such an accusation could take a dangerous turn for the Ahmadis. He proceeded straightaway to the office of the deputy superintendent of police to verify if such an incident had indeed occurred, or whether it was just rumour-mongering. And if it had taken place, had an initial report of the incident been filed? There it was confirmed for him that, no, it wasn't just a rumour. At noon, a man named Sarfaraz Husain, one of Noor Nagar's residents, had submitted a report that around 10 a.m. a man named Muhammad Ahmad was standing in the courtyard of the Ahmadiyyah temple (which they insisted on calling a mosque) and was setting fire to some Qurʾanic sheets. Munir Ahmad, Nabi Ahmad, Nasrullah and Naseruddin, all Ahmadis, were also standing in the courtyard of the temple, helping and egging him on. The submitter of the report also handed over some burned sheets of the Qurʾan, which he was able to salvage with difficulty, as evidence. He also stated that many such sheets lay scattered at the place in question. Besides Sarfaraz Husain, Muhammad Din, Ghulam Nabi and Rehmat Khan were present at the scene and had witnessed the entire episode with their own eyes. When Bashir Ahmad inquired about the deputy sahib, he was told that he had gone to Noor Nagar in his jeep, followed by twenty policemen and two thanedars from the district capital in a police lorry. The form the circumstances had taken, thanks to the sordid plot masterminded by the enemy, assured him of the total destruction that lay ahead. For a while he just stood there, stupefied and unable to think. He didn't know what to do for the preservation of the local Ahmadis now that the administration, the religious fanatics and Ahmadis' personal enemies had perpetrated such a frightful intrigue. Unknowingly, his steps took him to the assistant commissioner who happened still to be in his office. Without permission, he rushed into the office and said, 'Sir, the whole scheme to wipe out the local Ahmadis has now been exposed. One last time I've come to appeal to you in the name of humanity.'

'Chaudhry sahib, have a seat. You look quite worried. What happened exactly?'

'Our personal enemy Sarfaraz Husain has filed an FIR against us at the police station. We've described to you the whole story behind his animosity many times before and you know it well. According to this report, the Imam of the Noor Nagar Ahmadiyyah mosque was found standing in the courtyard of the mosque at 10 a.m. today setting fire to some pages of the Qur'an, and four very honourable and respectable Ahmadis, two of whom are senior citizens, were encouraging him to continue. Besides Sarfaraz Husain, there were three other eyewitnesses to the incident, all Sarfaraz Husain's personal employees. Can anyone with even the least bit of common sense believe such a story? The report was accepted without any investigation and the deputy sahib has proceeded to the place in question with twenty policemen and two officers so that if no disturbance had yet begun, he could help kick-start it. You can easily guess the intention of the police from this. Everyone knows that the Ahmadis regard the Holy Qur'an as the greatest blessing of God to mankind and know that only by following its teachings can they succeed in this world and the next. If five Ahmadis of impeccable piety would together set fire to the Qur'an on this day, what would they gain by it besides disgrace in this world and the next, and the immediate death and annihilation of the local Ahmadis to the last man, woman and child? You can imagine the calamity that will occur at the rally today when the preachers hand out this news in their own fashion to the crowd of thousands.'

Having spoken his mind, Bashir Ahmad got up and started walking towards the door. The AC exclaimed: 'Listen, Chaudhry sahib, I'll get on the wireless right this minute . . .'

'You go ahead and do what you will. God be with you!'

On his way home Bashir Ahmad passed through many bazaars and alleys. He felt that the attitude and manner of the town's residents was somewhat different that day. The praises of the Prophet were coming high and loud and without a break from the mosque's loudspeakers. Many stores were shut. There were fewer customers than usual in the bazaar. Compared to the other Fridays, there was a larger crowd today, all in freshly washed clothes, with spotless white caps on their heads and flip-flops on their feet as they moved gracefully towards the grand mosque. The second they hear this patently false news of the Qur'an burning, he began to think, these people will be transformed into a passionate, boiling, uncontrollable flood of hatred and anger, and surge forth to take their revenge. Their egotism will never allow them to tolerate a minority as small as an ant thumbing its nose at a majority as big as an elephant. There will certainly be all kinds of people—educated, bright and sober—in the crowd, but no one will attempt to verify the assertions thrown at them from the pulpit, nor wonder if it was even possible for any Ahmadi, given his beliefs, to commit such a heinous act. No, these simple-minded people won't go into such details; they'll jump into the crowd instead and fall ravenously upon a small settlement of innocent people to torch their houses and murder them with fearless impunity.

The bewilderment generated by the present state of affairs and dread of the consequences plunged Bashir Ahmad into a dark cave of hopelessness. For a few moments he stood at the side of a street stunned, like a statue. Then he called upon God in his heart and came to the realization that this was no time to sink into deep thoughts or speculate about the future. He knew he had to focus his thoughts on the immediate situation and make decisions based only on the exigencies of that situation. He decided he would make only one decision at a time and leave the rest to God. God would always do what is best for His creatures.

When Bashir Ahmad stepped into the house at about two, a frightened Mubashshir came up to him and started staring at him. He let Mubashshir drape himself against his legs and rubbed his head lovingly. Mubashshir's condition grieved him. He realized that they had failed to provide a sense of security for their children, a natural right at that age. He asked Amtul, 'Has there been any news from Noor Nagar?'

'No. Were you expecting any? I'll warm up the food for you.'

'No, don't. I don't have time for that. Has nobody come from Noor Nagar either?'

'No. Who were you expecting? You don't even have time for a meal? Is everything all right?'

'No. Nothing is all right. Someone has set fire to the Qur'an in Noor Nagar and pinned the blame on the Ahmadis. Now only God knows what will happen to the innocent people there.'

'This mischief has got to be the handiwork of Sarfaraz Husain. Who else could commit an act like that? Did you not inform the police?'

'It never came to that. The one who burned the Qur'an also went and filed an FIR against us. We knew nothing; what could we have reported? A police detachment has already gone to Noor Nagar headed by the deputy. If the place was still peaceful, it won't remain that way after their arrival. Here, the rally is in progress. You can hear it over the loudspeaker. Whoever is speaking now is accusing the Ahmadis non-stop and hurling lies about them. In a couple of hours we'll find out whether the menace will turn in the direction of our street or towards Noor Nagar. My guess is that because of the incident, it'll move towards Noor Nagar. The local population there would never agree to terrorizing the Ahmadis, or looting or torching their houses. They would have to get mercenaries from outside for that. But maybe not, the fired-up students at the rally will start marching to Noor Nagar on their own. Right now I must go call Master Lateef and the other dignitaries of the street to my office to tell them about the recent developments. Then they can decide what steps to take next.'

Everyone was at home and got together at his call. Bashir Ahmad told them everything he knew about the incident at Noor Nagar and added that, in his view, an immediate reaction was more likely to take place there rather than in their own street. Besides their own security, they had to think of how to help the Ahmadis in Noor Nagar. The audience was struck dumb as soon as Bashir Ahmad had finished speaking. No one said anything. The terrible din of the speech going on at the rally had circumscribed the entire silent room like a thundering, rushing monsoon cloud. It was as if the little birds, their heads stuck under tree branches and their turbulent hearts beating fast and furious in a violent storm, were now face-to-face with the demon of death and destruction aiming to stagger them with its roar.

Finally, Master Lateef broke the long silence. He spoke as if he were talking to himself: 'Who could possibly have imagined that Sarfaraz Husain would fall so low as to burn the Qur'an and lay the blame at our door just to grab a few kanals of land to which he is in no way entitled! As regards the problems of the Noor Nagar Ahmadis and how we can help them, nothing can be decided until someone from there comes and lets us know.'

Bashir Ahmad said, 'Instead of waiting for someone to come from there, why don't we send someone from here to find out about the situation there?'

'But if there's really trouble there, wouldn't our man be walking right into it?' Taj Bibi's husband, Anwaar Ahmad, remarked, and added, 'He might even lose his life.'

'Let's send Ismail, the pharmacy man,' Bashir Ahmad suggested. Later, as an afterthought, he added, 'But he's too old. He may not be up to such a nerve-racking expedition. I think it would be better to send Chauhan. He's a journalist, so no policeman would question him. Let me go and talk to him.'

'I'm not at all in favour of sending anyone who doesn't belong to the Ahmadi community,' Master Lateef voiced his objection.

Everybody supported Master Lateef and Bashir Ahmad's proposal was shot down, so he observed, 'Trust is a two-way street, never one-way. Ismail and Chauhan both hold very clear views about life that do not allow any partiality or prejudice. As regards religion, they both uphold the total freedom of the individual and are against state interference. I am fully aware of their qualities and limitations. If we trust them today in this minor matter, we may well expect some positive action from them tomorrow. It's due to this lack of mutual trust that we're under the dark clouds of oppression and nobody comes forward to speak on our behalf about truth and justice. Thousands of people are at the rally. They're listening to baseless accusations against us and believing them. And all because of the trust, though eminently misplaced in this case, the speakers have created in them.'

'To begin with, the issue isn't a minor one,' countered Master Lateef. 'Secondly, this is not the time to try new experiments. It would be better if you set them aside for another, more appropriate time.'

Again everyone affirmed his argument, and again Bashir Ahmad had to remain quiet.

'You hear the sounds blaring out of the loudspeakers, don't you?' Muhammad Sharif pointed out. 'Even if you ignore the speakers' condemnation of the Ahmadis, at least you can easily infer from the thundering, noisy response of the mob that there must be thousands of people in the audience. As soon as they hear the news about the Qur'an burning, their relentless torrent is going to wash away the few houses on this street like straw.'

In an attempt to allay his fears, Bashir Ahmad said, 'Muhammad Sharif sahib, don't get so worked up. Have faith in God and His succour. Didn't He keep Noah's ark safe in the flood? Didn't He make the swallows defeat an army of elephants? Fear is an infectious disease; a person catches it easily from others. Keep your wits and courage about you. This is a time of trial; God willing, it will end well for us.'

'The residents of the few Ahmadi houses scattered in different areas of the town have all locked their doors and left this morning,' Lateef informed the group. 'Good for them. At least their lives will be safe and since their houses are located inside other localities, they won't be torched, perhaps only looted. When they come back, they'll at least have a roof over their heads, which is not the case for us: our houses will surely be looted as well as burned, and we might even lose our lives if we stay here. There's no guarantee that we'll be able to save our honour either. Why don't we abandon our houses before the rally ends? As planned, every house has prepared for departure. The women have already packed their valuables and their burqas are ready to be donned. The doors of the last two houses of the street that open on to the fields have been left unlocked, and doors that open into the street are ready to be locked from the inside. Within five minutes of a decision to evacuate, a population of eighty-nine individuals will be out in the open fields.'

'And then, where do we go?' asked Anwaar Ahmad. 'We had decided to leave for Noor Nagar in an eventuality. Now that doesn't look safe. So where do we head off to now?'

'The decision about where and how a family will proceed will have to be made individually by the head of each household,' Master Lateef offered. 'My own view is that a neighbourhood in any village, town or city where there is hope of getting shelter will do. Right now, this town and Noor Nagar are under threat. The rest of the country should be comparatively safe. As soon as peace is restored, we'll return to our homes.'

Ahmad Din added in a low tone, 'If they're still there!'

Lateef looked at his face closely; then, with a bitter smile, he exclaimed, 'Right you are, sir!'

Bashir Ahmad suddenly spoke up. 'No, no, Master sahib. It shouldn't be this way. The responsibility for some families will have to be assumed by others. For example, I'll take Masi Jannat and Munawwar with me. Muhammad Sharif's mother is paralytic and can't take a step on her own at all. His children are small, he can't carry them all alone. We'll have to decide right now who will help in the transportation of such families. Young men should volunteer their services for such work. Right now you should make a separate duty roster for each young man and make him understand in detail what he's expected to do. Anwaar sahib, please take a pen and paper, and make a list of the young men.' Then he addressed Master Lateef, 'If we can evacuate the whole population in five minutes, we still have plenty of time. The entrance to the street has a strong iron gate. It will take the mob some time to break it down or scale it. Besides that, the houses will be locked from the inside. We'll have about half an hour before the mob gets into the street and starts entering our houses. By that time, we'll be easily out into the fields and on our way to our various destinations. Only then will the mob be able to get inside the houses. If we leave right now, it will be like asking for trouble. Have some patience and wait. It's possible we may not have to vacate our houses at all. In the meanwhile, we'll find out what the situation is in Noor Nagar.'

Thinking about the situation, Noor Ahmad wondered aloud, 'The FIR was filed at noon. Now it's half past four. No one has come from Noor Nagar to give us any report.'

Muhammad Sharif said, 'They must be trapped in their own misery. Who would come to tell us?'

'If we inquire from the police station, we'll certainly find out something or the other about the situation there,' Bashir Ahmad observed. 'That would make it easier to come to some decision about how to move people over.'

'The rally is still going on,' Lateef said. 'The ones who aren't inside the meeting hall are split into small groups and are standing here and there in the street, talking. The atmosphere must be getting heated up against the Ahmadis. It would be dangerous for an Ahmadi to even step out of this street, let alone head off to the police station. The second someone from Sultanpur points him out, the fanatics from out of town will make short work of him.'

'All right,' Bashir Ahmad gave in, 'we'll wait.' Then he addressed everyone. 'Did you notice the trickery of the administration? Since this morning, they have entrusted three policemen to the security of this street. What security can three policemen provide if the mob turns this way? They'll turn tail the minute they see the mob. There's one thing, though; if some new policemen have come on duty, they might perhaps have some news of Noor Nagar.'

He got up and looked out. The same three policemen

on duty in the morning had closed the iron gate and sat behind it smoking in the street. In the meantime, the people gathered in Bashir Ahmad's office heard the Imam and chief preacher of Sultanpur's Jamia Mosque screaming into the loudspeaker, 'The enemies of God and the followers of a false prophet have set fire to the Qur᾿an in Noor Nagar. They have challenged the lovers of the Prophet and the guardians of the sanctity of the Qur᾿an. It is imperative upon every Muslim to reach Noor Nagar right now and punish these enemies of Islam. One hundred staff-bearing students, their shrouds tied around their heads, are ready to set off for Noor Nagar. Join them and live up to your religious obligation.' No sooner had he finished than a tumultuous noise rose from the meeting hall. For many minutes thereafter, the air vibrated with the ear-splitting slogans of 'Go, Go, Go to Noor Nagar.' When the loudspeakers were turned off, it seemed to the people in Bashir Ahmad's office as if a sudden crushing silence had engulfed them, and that what they had just heard wasn't reality but a hallucination or nightmare. During the preacher's announcement and slogans, they were gripped by a feeling of stark terror and silently stared helplessly at each other's faces with questioning looks. Then they began evading each other's eyes and a strange embarrassment overtook them. Meanwhile, Rehmat Ilahi from Noor Nagar entered the room perspiring heavily and, after greeting them, said, 'It took me three hours to do this one-hour journey. Lord, with what difficulty have I gotten here! I had to walk through the fields!'

A volley of questions rained down on him to tell them the whole story.

'Wait a little,' Bashir Ahmad said to the man. 'Take a drink of water and catch your breath first. Then we'll talk.'

After his perspiration had dried, Bashir Ahmad asked him, 'How did the incident of the burning of the Qur'anic pages take place? And who did it?'

'Nobody knows who did it or how. Around noon, when Maulvi Mahmood Ahmad opened the mosque for the Juma prayer, he saw some half-burned sheets of the Qur'an flying about in the courtyard. He gathered them, put them in a plastic bag and placed them above the spare copies of the Qur'an in the cupboard. Meanwhile, people started coming in for the prayer. Whoever came in had a few partially burned pages in his hands. When I got there, I saw a dozen young men walking around the mosque, on maulvi sahib's orders, collecting the scattered half-burned sheets and putting them in plastic bags. I joined them. We picked up each and every sheet. We were all wondering what kind of crazy person would do such a thing, certainly no one in his right mind would. None of us even considered the possibility that it could be part of a conspiracy against us. We all agreed that some kid had happened upon a box of matches and a sheaf of some old pages from the Qur'an and just indulged in his passion for setting fire to paper. Around one-thirty, while the sermon was still in progress, the police surrounded the mosque. A deputy and two thanedars entered the mosque. Maulvi Muhammad Ahmad, Nabi Ahmad, Nasrullah and Naseruddin were handcuffed and handed over to two policemen who put them into the police van. When they searched the mosque, all they could find were the half-burned pages of the Qur'an inside the cupboard and they took those into their custody. A temporary police post has been set up in the village and it has been announced that anyone who steps out of his house before 5 a.m. will be shot. Gun-toting policemen are patrolling the streets. I have no knowledge of what happened after that. I came to inform you folks.'

'The rioters must have set out for Noor Nagar by now,' said Bashir Ahmad, thinking. 'How they're treated when they get there, or what they do to the Ahmadis, will depend on the behaviour of the police. Anyway, our first job is to arrange for the bail of the four who have been arrested and see in what direction the police will attempt to take the investigation. If it supports Sarfaraz Husain and his claim, then we must file a protest with the local, district and provincial officials and do it in a timely manner. We must communicate to them immediately every attempt of the miscreants to twist the facts.'

After he had gone that far, the policemen guarding the street knocked at the office door. When they were called in, one of them said to Bashir Ahmad, 'Sir, the rally is over. Nobody has dared to come this way. By God's grace the whole street and its residents are perfectly safe. We would have confronted them if they had dared. Even now, if there's any service we can render, let us know.'

Bashir Ahmad asked, 'Were you given food and refreshments on time?'

'Yes, sir. You've been very kind. We were well looked after.'

Bashir Ahmad said to Master Lateef, 'Master-ji, please give each one of them a hundred rupees.'

When the money had been handed out, Bashir Ahmad said to them, 'We thank you very much. You have our permission to leave.'

After the policemen had left, Bashir Ahmad suggested, 'I think Anwaar Ahmad should go out on his bicycle and get some news of the situation in the city, whether there's peace and quiet or whether there's been any change on account of the rally and the news of the burning of the Qur'an. And also, Anwaar sahib, I don't think it would be wise for you to venture into the area of the Jamia Mosque. Participants from distant areas and students from neighbouring towns will still be there. They won't start leaving until tomorrow.'

With the departure of the policemen and Anwaar Ahmad, and the disappearance of tension from the faces of the dignitaries, everyone felt that the danger of immediate riots had been postponed and that things were returning to normal. Now everyone started to make some excuse to get up and leave. Finally, only Bashir Ahmad, Master Lateef, Muhammad Hanif and Rehmat Ali from Noor Nagar were left in the office.

'The news of the Qur'an burning and the imposition of a curfew in Noor Nagar,' Bashir Ahmad began, 'won't take long to spread throughout the country. It may echo even in the halls of the provincial and central governments and instructions will be issued demanding immediate action for the preservation of peace. If this not very well-known place becomes the centre of everyone's attention, it's very likely that rioting may not erupt in Sultanpur after all.'

'I don't agree,' Master Lateef said. 'Aren't you assuming too much? It won't take much for the local administration to create trouble and then come up with the excuse that the public became so enraged by the Ahmadis burning the Qur'an that all their efforts to control them failed.'

Bashir Ahmad considered that for a while and then said, 'Yes, Master sahib, that is also possible. In the end, everything hinges upon the intention of the local officials.'

Meanwhile, Anwaar Ahmad returned from his tour of the town. 'The stores and streets are all open,' he informed them, 'and people are busy with their usual occupations. There's no obstruction anywhere. The educated, informed people think that someone has exploited the rally to launch a veritable campaign of hostility against the Ahmadis. But such people aren't too numerous and even though they'll call a spade a spade, they won't take any practical step in support of their view. Some people are terrified by the incident of the burning and are sure God's wrath will now descend upon them. Many are just standing around, totally stunned, asking each other in hushed tones, "Why in the world did the Ahmadis do such a thing?" But I didn't see anyone in a rage or stirred up. The four Ahmadis arrested and brought here from Noor Nagar are in the police lock-up. I didn't see them; I just gathered information about them and came back.'

'Shouldn't we perhaps send them food and other necessary things?' Rehmat Ali suggested.

'Don't worry,' Bashir Ahmad assured him. 'Everything will be taken care of, but we still need to find out what transpired in Noor Nagar after you left. Guess I'll have to go myself to find out.'

'Bashir sahib, did you think carefully about what Anwaar Ahmad just said?' Master Lateef asked. 'What I gathered from it is this: the people who come together and make a crowd, namely, the public, are straddling the fence at the moment. If someone incites them, they'll get up and go along with him and do whatever right or wrong he makes them do. But if someone told them the real facts, they would step down from the fence and quietly head home. We have no means to communicate our views to them, nor can we get in touch with them indirectly. There's no one around to talk to them on our behalf either. I don't know any. Do you? Even if there were such a person, there hasn't been that much understanding between him and us to make him believe what we say. Nor has any attempt ever been made to create such understanding. Who can we look to, to come forward in such critical circumstances and explain our point of view, to tear up the curtain of lies and have the courage to tell the truth? He should be someone the townsfolk trust and believe. So, under circumstances such as these, all we can do is depend on the administration. If the administration desires, Sultanpur can remain safe, but don't we already know which way they're inclined? Now as for the government's secret instructions about us, well, we have no inkling of them yet. Chances are they wouldn't be in our favour either. Perhaps it's under the cover of the same instructions that the deputy has been helping his friends. And the AC, as you already know, is a weak man.'

'Master sahib,' Bashir Ahmad answered, 'your analysis is perfect. We and the public suffer from a lack of mutual trust; nonetheless most ordinary people usually stay in a neutral position. There are plenty of people in every town and city who consider religious strife such as this a danger to the peace and well-being of the country and are against those who start it. But they're not organized. Not long ago, I offered a proposal in this connection, but it was rejected. Anyway, to depend entirely upon the administration to guard the property, life and honour of some eighty or ninety people would be putting all our eggs in one basket. And you're quite familiar with the chameleon-like character of the administration. It can't be trusted.'

'I hope you won't mind if I say that your proposal was turned down with good reason,' Master Lateef quickly remarked. 'It was an entirely different matter. It had to do with communicating information upon which other decisions were to be based. Entrusting someone inexperienced and unconcerned with this sort of matter could have been dangerous. Now you're talking about trying to establish contact with the public. In that regard, it would be good if the people you trust do succeed. And even if they don't, because of being incapable or ill intentioned, there won't be much damage. The situation will stay as it is. It won't deteriorate further.'

'Master sahib, how can you expect any positive results if those wishing to inspire trust themselves begin without it,' Bashir Ahmad argued. 'Anyway, I'll go and talk to Ismail and Chauhan. Let's see what help they can give us in the matter.'

It was already dark when Bashir Ahmad reached Ismail's store. The lights had already come on in the bazaar. Then again, not many customers showed up in the main bazaars of Sultanpur in the evening. It was the same that day. This lack of bustle and activity wasn't due to the rally; it was a matter of daily routine. Alone, lost in his thoughts, Ismail was taking papers out of the table drawer and examining them, as though looking for something in particular. Bashir's greeting startled him. He looked at him, smiled and said, 'Arre, Bashir sahib, you? You really shouldn't have come out this way today.'

'The rally is over and done with. What's to worry about now? Even if I had come out during the rally, no one in Sultanpur would have dared raise his hand to me—you know that. Where is your "gang"? They didn't get together today?'

'Shaikh Sardar Ali and the Haji were both at the rally. Afterwards they must have gone home tired. Ahmad and Sufi were here, but the loudspeakers were so noisy you could hardly carry on a conversation. Disgusted, they finally left too. Chauhan didn't show up today. I don't know where he's disappeared.'

'Ismail sahib, is there a way to inform people that the goal of this rally was not to safeguard a particular religious viewpoint, that it was a squabble over a few kanals of land between two people, one of whom, unfortunately, happened to be an Ahmadi. That's what transformed a molehill into a mountain, and threw the lives and property of hundreds of people into jeopardy. Had the two parties been of the same faith, the matter would never have gone beyond the courts, and ordinary people wouldn't have become involved. What ignited the gunpowder was actually the difference between the beliefs of the parties. The incident of the Qur'an burning is indeed regrettable, but it's still a link in the same chain. The truth about that is also hidden from the public. The public needs to know who those people are and the ends they were pursuing that has resulted in the commission of such a beastly act.'

'Who did such a crazy thing—do you know?'

Bashir Ahmad told Ismail whatever details he knew at that time and repeated: How do you inform people of the truth so their anger cools down?

'Isn't this precisely the duty of the newspapers?' Ismail said. He added, 'But I don't think any newspaper, not even at the national level, can be persuaded to show enough courage to go against the policies of the well-organized religious parties and publish the explanation you've given.'

'If Chauhan could publish these details in his weekly, at least our position would become clear to the local population and they would see how groundless their complaint against us is.'

'This week's issue is already out. It'll be distributed tomorrow so nothing new can be included. The next issue will be out in a week. By that time whatever is to happen will have happened and any after-the-fact explanation would be pointless. Again, if you ask me, it would be difficult for Chauhan to publish it. I doubt if he would go against the wishes of the AC and the police. You're already familiar with the trust he enjoys with the town's important people. If he tells the truth, people will say he sold out and is telling lies. And given his reputation, his readers will believe this immediately. That would harm your case more than help it.

'Another way would be to stand at the corner of the main bazaar or in some crowded chowk and have someone state the facts briefly and truthfully, without dressing them up. This isn't a big city, you know. Just two or three speeches of this sort and every child in town would know the true facts. It would be difficult for any preacher afterwards to exploit anyone emotionally merely by the strength of his lies, or persuade them to become willing tools for his selfish motives.'

'There's only a danger until the out-of-towners, especially the students herded here in large numbers, have left. Now, in such a short time, how and where will you find a person who's trusted by people and whose words are believable?'

Looking straight into Ismail's eyes, in an attempt to appeal to him, Bashir Ahmad said to him with all gravity, 'Instead of looking elsewhere, Ismail sahib, I suggest you yourself give it a try.'

Ismail erupted in a hearty laugh. 'Chaudhry sahib,' he said, 'you couldn't be more simple-minded! It's one thing to sit in a chair within the four walls of your own store and broadcast your views, and quite another to stand in front of a hostile mob and talk it into changing its beliefs. I wish I had that kind of skill, but I don't. And also, please remember one thing: don't ever let your vanity get the better of you to try such a thing yourself, or even allow anyone from your jamaʿat to try. Before you had so much as opened your mouth you would be physically assaulted and violently removed from the premises. I've been watching the conduct of religious hatred since 1947. It's only waiting for an excuse to flare up; once it does, it spreads everywhere like wildfire.'

Deep lines of despair cut into the faces of both men. They sat quietly for a long time, each sunk in his own thoughts. At last Bashir Ahmad stood up, saying, 'So, there's no other option now except to look towards a dishonest administration.'

'Yes, that's just what the situation demands.'

On his way home Bashir Ahmad was thinking that in his haste he had tried to work miracles. Such a job required careful planning. To attempt to do something quickly that by its nature demanded a much longer time was plain stupidity. True, a stitch in time does save nine, but sitting forever waiting to apply a stitch where there is neither a rip nor even any cloth is equally stupid. To grow a mustard crop, you must first prepare the ground, then plant the seeds, and then wait four months while you water the land and take care of it. First the plants will raise their tiny heads; then slowly, after some time they'll take the shape of the crop itself. The impatience of one's desires can't force the plants out of the earth sooner.

Along the way, he ran into many acquaintances. Some just greeted him and kept going. Some he shook hands with. With some he even inquired about their welfare and with others he had rather lengthy conversations. Everyone's attitude was normal; he couldn't detect anything unusual. 'Would these people kill me because my religious belief isn't the same as theirs?' he wondered. 'No, they would never do that. I mustn't allow mistrust to creep into my heart. They're nice, simple-hearted folks, but like all simple-hearted folks, easily deceived. But then, we haven't done anything to save them from deception either. If we had, long ago, prepared them mentally for the kind of crisis they're facing today, I wouldn't be having the apprehensions I have now.' When he left Ismail's company, he was quite disheartened by Ismail's refusal and by the blow Ismail had delivered to his own vanity. Now, though, he could see that Ismail was right in what he said, that what he said was based on facts. In this unsettled time, Ismail wasn't trying to dodge anything. He had carefully analysed every aspect of the issue and shown him how his proposal was unworkable at this time.

As he approached his street he saw that the gate closed in the morning was still closed, even padlocked from the inside. When he called out his son Mubashshir's name, a young man from the roof of the house next to his own responded, 'Uncle, I'm coming down.'

The young man opened one half of the iron gate just a wee bit and quickly closed it again, and secured the gate with the padlock after Bashir Ahmad entered.

'This is a good thing you fellows are doing,' he said.

'Master sahib has ordered the gate to remain closed and locked at all times. He has asked one alert young man to stand guard on the roof of each of the four corner houses of the street. The watch will be maintained until morning in four-hour shifts. The duty roster has been set up. At midnight Aslam will take my place. I'll hand the key to the gate over to him and go to sleep. At four, he'll wake me and go to sleep himself.'

'Where is Master sahib?'

'Sir, he's having his supper.'

Hearing the word supper, he suddenly felt his own need for food. He turned towards his own door, saying, 'Son, ask him to visit me in my office when he's finished eating.'

A frightened Mubashshir opened the door and scanned his father's face despondently. Bashir Ahmad patted him on his head. In the light of a single bulb in the courtyard, some women wrapped in white dupattas sat quietly on three cots with their heads hung low, immersed in thought. Bashir Ahmad recognized his wife, his sister, Masi and Taj Bibi, but couldn't identify the other two women. After greeting his sister, he told her, 'Nasira, please bring my food to my office.'

Masi said, 'Son Bashir Ahmad, we're about to leave. Come here and eat out in the open. It must be hot in your office.'

'It's not a problem, Masi. You stay. I've got to be in my office anyway.'

'Son, tell us just one thing. How long is this trouble going to last? I've locked Munawwar in his room since yesterday morning. You know he's a free-flying bird. I don't think he can take this imprisonment much longer. He weeps bitterly, and when he does, I start to cry with him. What can I do? My heart breaks seeing him in this condition.'

'Masi, if you could just somehow get through this one more day, everything will be all right afterwards. Munawwar will be able to roam the town freely as he did before and there won't be any danger to him.'

Taj Bibi, feeling helpless because of the circumstances and after a great deal of hesitation, slipped her dupatta over her forehead and pulled it down even lower with her hands. For the first time in her life she finally mustered the courage to address Bashir Ahmad directly: 'Brother, what's going to happen to us? I'm exhausted thinking about it. I can understand nothing, nor does anyone tell me anything. Why is it that people have so suddenly become thirsty for our blood? What wrong have we done? Where are we going to go this time if we are uprooted yet again?'

'Sister, today was the most difficult day of all. By God's grace it has passed without incident. We can expect some danger until tomorrow afternoon. If that passes in peace and quiet, it will all be well again, God willing. Please don't be too worried.'

'How can I not? You wouldn't know, but our whole lives we've denied ourselves even little things to arrange all the necessities for the dowries of our two daughters. The wedding date is only fifteen days away. If some wretched ones rob us of their dowries, what are we going to do? How will we send off our daughters?' She hid her face in her dupatta and began crying.

'Sister Taj Bibi, have some courage. Crying won't solve anything. We had nothing at all when we arrived here, we left behind everything we owned for fear of the Sikhs. We were penniless. Now, by God's grace, we hardly lack anything. Don't lose heart. The toughest time is already over. Tomorrow will also pass peacefully.' Bashir Ahmad's voice rose a little as he spoke.

Meanwhile, one of the two newly arrived women said, 'For six months my old mother has lain in bed. Her health is so precarious that she's almost at her last breath.'

'All the necessary arrangements are in place. If, God forbid, there's an assault, the young men who've been assigned that duty will take her out on a cot.'

'As far as the bus station, fine. What will we do after that? How would we proceed from there? Mother isn't even fit to travel by bus or train.' She began crying and said through her weeping, 'The neighbours on the street won't let us leave now. They say that if we leave, it will start a stampede: everyone will abandon their houses and run. And a stampede, as you know, would surely invite an attack. Our houses will be looted and torched. Tell us what we should do. Had we left earlier, we'd have borne whatever loss was our fate, but at least we could have taken our mother away to die in some decent place. Who knows when the enemy will come charging in.'

'How can anyone predict when the enemy is going to be here, or if he's going to be here at all? Maybe he relishes it more by dangling us on the gallows. What's he going to do when he arrives? Will plundering our houses satisfy him or will he also need to burn them? Will he be happy killing us or would he much rather see us writhing in pain and agony? His one obvious and clear objective is to make us so miserable that we abandon our faith in desperation. That's not going to happen. We'll give up our lives, but not our faith.'

The woman sensed irascibility and a hiss of anger in his voice. She looked at his face once in astonishment and then started weeping and sobbing loudly. Amtul got up, wrapped her arms around her and comforted her lovingly.

All of a sudden Masi spoke up authoritatively, 'Bashir

Ahmad! Relax! Have some patience, son. Cooped up inside the house, we suffer more than you do. Our troubles and difficulties have become as big as mountains, which you know nothing about. Perhaps all this running around sustains your heart a bit, getting good news and bad, discovering what's happening or is likely to. But for us, days and nights have stretched to infinity. Then there are these frightening thoughts that crowd our minds, the lurking fears that weigh on our hearts. When they totally suffocate us, we run here helplessly in the hope that we may find some means of solace. We don't come to bother you.'

'You're right, Masi. Actually, I'm feeling quite tired. Perhaps I couldn't control my voice. God has brought us so far under His protection. The danger exists only for a few more hours. That too shall pass, by His grace. Please don't let yourself worry too much.'

Then Bashir Ahmad spoke to the woman whom he hadn't met before. 'Bibi . . . sister, please don't be sad. Tomorrow morning, after the Fajr prayer, in whatever way possible, I'll arrange for you and your mother to leave here safely.'

Masi called out, 'Nasira beti, bring your brother his meal!'

'Masi, I've laid it out in his office.'

Master Lateef began telling Bashir Ahmad, 'Rehmat Ali and I took food over to the police station.'

'Good, but did you get to see the detainees?'

'Yes, we did. Well, it was just a matter of a few rupees, anyway.' Both of them began to laugh.

'I'm worried about Uncle Nabi Ahmad and Brother Nasrullah. They're both quite old. At this age they should be resting and taking it easy, not going through some horrific detention in this miserably hot weather.'

'Arre, Chaudhry sahib, what do you take them for? They're full of vigour and courage. They've already had their first run-in with the thanedar.'

'How's that?'

'When the call for the Maghrib prayer was heard, our people asked Maulvi Muhammad Ahmad to lead the prayer and lined up behind him. The thanedar passed by them and stopped. He said, "The Ahmadis are not allowed to pray in the open. What you're doing is against the law. Stop the prayer right now." But they kept it up. When they had finished, he came again and said, "I warned you but you didn't stop. I'll have to register a challan against you." Whereupon Uncle Nabi Ahmad blurted out, "A while ago we performed our Asr prayer here. And we'll also perform our Isha prayer here. Your coercive laws mean nothing in the eyes of God. So long as we're here, you may lodge five challans a day against us. We don't care."'

'Then?'

'Then we don't know whether he filed the challans or not. Perhaps he gave up the idea, considering the amount of paperwork involved. When they offered their Isha prayer, the thanedar was there in the police station, but he didn't raise any objection.'

'I wish they hadn't made all that fuss with the present situation. Anyway, tell me, did you get any fresh news of Noor Nagar?'

'We inquired from the scribe at the police station, but at that time no good or bad news about Noor Nagar had come to light, so we guessed that the curfew was still on and it was quiet there. Perhaps no news itself could be taken as good news.'

'Master sahib, it was announced on the loudspeaker that a hundred students have left town. Even if no one from the local population joined them, a hundred club-carrying students is a sizeable number. They can create havoc if they're bent on harming thirty or forty unarmed Ahmadis confined to their homes. The wonder is, though, where have they gone? Perhaps the police officers thought that if anything happened in Noor Nagar during the curfew, the responsibility would fall squarely on them and they would have a hard time explaining it away so they may have cancelled the entire plan of assault and plunder. Now, how can we know if the students were stopped before they left or if they were asked to turn back midway? The DSP's main objective was to teach Munir Ahmad a lesson and send a warning to the Ahmadis of Noor Nagar. That has been accomplished. Let's hope nothing untoward will happen there now.'

'If they can't do anything in Noor Nagar because of the constraints of the circumstances, I hope they don't turn up here in the morning to punish us instead.'

'I doubt if that would happen. Had Noor Nagar been a town rather than a village, the rally would have taken place there. Sultanpur's misfortune is that it's the only big town in Noor Nagar's vicinity so they were naturally forced to choose it for the rally. The real target of the DSP was Noor Nagar. That whole incident of the Qur'an burning was just a ruse to turn people's attention in that direction.'

Undone by the day's heat, fatigue and worry, Bashir Ahmad finally fell on his bed in the courtyard at 11 p.m., but couldn't fall asleep. In every which way, the more he tried to force himself to sleep, the more it shunned him. He told himself countless times that whatever shape circumstances were going to assume tomorrow morning must surely have solidified in the womb of time by now. His worrying about it wouldn't change anything; it would only make him more nervous. The mind has its own modus operandi, its own logic. If it was ever contented with what the tongue told it, it would court its own disaster. Whatever step it would take next must first be measured against its own touchstone of what is good or bad for it. And if ever caught in a state of indecision, it keeps both body and soul in a state of relentless tension.

Tired of constantly tossing and turning on the cot, Bashir Ahmad sat up. Amtul and Mubashshir were sound asleep on the cot next to his. He felt envious of their sleep. Then he thought: who knows, with their nerves frayed by fear they might suddenly wake up from horrid dreams and feel envious of his sleeplessness. Treading softly, he walked up the stairs to the open roof. Mahmood, a distant nephew, was standing guard. The other boy, Siddiq, had finished with his duty at midnight and was now sleeping on the cot. The atmosphere was close and muggy as a result of heavy rains on the distant mountains. The moon, nibbled on one side like a child's stale flatbread, glowed feebly as if through a dusty glass. A weary silence and the pale moonlight spread all around. Beyond the closed gate of the street, the trees stood still and looked like their own shadows. Towards the bazaar side of the street, the chain of haphazard interconnected houses was so quiet that it resembled the ruins of some devastated city, not a place where humans lived. In a few places, the faint glow of electric bulbs inside their hanging blue fixtures was too feeble to light up anything besides the surrounding silence.

At first Mahmood was surprised to see him, but then he

thought that Bashir Ahmad must have come to check on whether he was remiss in his watchman's duty. He went up close to Bashir Ahmad and spoke very quietly, as if taking care lest the silence be stirred up by his voice and crash and scatter everywhere, informing the enemy of their secret watch. The enemy might use this knowledge against them—might even send them to their deaths.

'Uncle, go and rest. Working all day must have tired you. You can rest assured I won't fall asleep while on duty.'

Bashir Ahmad smiled on hearing that. 'No, son, I haven't come to nose around. I just couldn't sleep. It's so miserably muggy downstairs, so I thought I'd come up. No one would behave irresponsibly during this difficult time, I know. This would have disastrous consequences for everyone. You're a very cautious young man even under normal circumstances. How could you possibly go to sleep while on duty?'

One of Mahmood's ardent wishes was to be like Bashir Ahmad. Hearing his praises, his neck stiffened a little and a smile of pride and gratefulness crept over his lips. Walking along the wall which served as a cover against detection, turning in all directions, lifting himself on his toes, he watched over the very depressing night and the even more desolate moonlight for a long time wondering whether he had raised his toes to look outside or to peek inside himself. Perhaps he was that night, or that night was him. Once, in the distance, he heard the faint bark of a dog. It seemed to come from inside the well of the night, the last yelp of a canine before drowning. In the senseless quiet of an indifferent desert, the bark was the dog's last desperate attempt to feel some remnant of life before the darkness closed in on him. Then a thought flitted across his mind: What if the farmers had watered the fields we had designated for our escape? It would be one hell of a job making the women and children wade through mud.

'What time is it now, Mahmood?' Bashir Ahmad asked.

The young man looked at his watch and said, 'Quarter to three, Uncle.'

'Yes, I remember. There is something for you to do.'

'Tell me.'

'After the Fajr prayer both you and Siddiq should go to the stand and get a comfortable cab for Lahore. You know Safia Bibi, Abdul Rashid's wife—she wants to take her sick mother to Lahore. Get her carefully seated in the cab. The driver will drop them off wherever they want to go in Lahore. Fix the fare with the driver. Take the money from me and pay him in advance.'

'Will do, Uncle, just as you wish. Be assured.'

Bashir Ahmad had just turned to go back down when he heard someone call from near the iron gate, 'Bashir sahib, Chaudhry Bashir sahib!'

Bashir and Mahmood looked at each other as if asking who it could be. Bashir Ahmad peeked over the restraining wall. He saw four men standing in the bazaar outside the locked gate.

'Who is it, brother?'

'Rehmat Ilahi's younger brother Mushtaq Ali from Noor Nagar. I've got three other boys from Noor Nagar with me.'

'Is everything all right?'

'We'll tell you when you let us in.'

Within five minutes every house on the street was awake. Voices were heard. Lights came on. It seemed like *sehri* time during the month of Ramadan. Bashir Ahmad opened the door to his office and seated the young men. Within minutes a crowd of men of every age, young and old, gathered in the room. Rehmat Ilahi and Master Lateef also walked in. Mushtaq Ali and his three companions, none of whom was more than fourteen or fifteen, were so nervous and scared that they found it difficult to describe the incidents in a continuous coherent manner. In the middle of one thing, they would jump to something else.

'Tell us,' Bashir Ahmad asked Mushtaq Ali, 'did anyone die, ours or theirs?'

'No.'

'Thank God. At least that's comforting news. Now tell us, was anyone injured?'

'Yeah, they torched everything we had.'

'Answer only the questions I ask. Things will come later.'

'Yes, there are injuries.'

'On our side or theirs, or both?'

'Only on our side.'

'Who and how?'

Mushtaq Ali looked at his brother Rehmat Ilahi, as if he alone could understand his words, and said, 'Towards the west of the village . . . at the edge of the settlement . . . inside the street . . . the lone Ahmadi house, you know, Ghulam Ali Kashmiri's—the man who drives Uncle Munir Ahmad's tractor and whose family came from somewhere else to settle here . . .'

'Fine, fine, Mushtaq Ali. Go on. What happened to them?'

'The club-wielding fellows got to their house first. They forced them to open the door and kicked and slapped them. Then they threw all their belongings out into the street, poured some kerosene over the pile and set it on fire. You know Ghulam Ali's wife, Sakina? At first, she just stood near the burning stuff and cried. Then she began pulling and dragging things out of the fire. At that, one man hit her hard on her back with his club. She fell into the fire face down. Ghulam Ali pulled her out and started pouring dirt on her clothes to put the fire out. Now they're bringing her here on the potter's cart.'

'What were you doing so far away from your house?' Bashir asked.

'I didn't go there.'

'So, who told you all this?'

Looking towards one of his companions, he said, 'This is Amjad. He's Ghulam Ali's son. He told us all this as we were coming here.'

When Bashir Ahmad looked at Amjad, he saw the boy had both of his hands on his face, and was crying and sobbing inconsolably. Rehmat Ilahi got up, pressed Amjad to his chest, kissed him and comforted him.

'Mushtaq Ali, it would be better if you told us just your own story,' Bashir Ahmad said. 'Just forget what happened to others and how. Tell us how you came to know about the attack.'

'What attack? There wasn't any. No cannons were fired, no bombs fell.'

'Okay. Forget about the attack. Just tell us what happened to you.'

'Our Noor Nagar mosque is located towards the east, a short distance from the street. There is some vacant land around it. The mosque itself would be about fifty *karams* from our house. There are three other Ahmadi houses near ours. They're joined to each other. In front there is a road and there is farmland behind. The other houses are on the left and right, at some distance.'

Becoming impatient, Bashir Ahmad said testily, 'We know the location and the geography of your house. Tell us the story. What happened and how?'

'I was asleep with my family outside in the courtyard when, around eleven, my Maa-ji woke me up and said, "Look, there are flames rising from the area of the mosque." My father and I wanted to check the flames, to see what they were about and where they were rising from. If the mosque was really on fire, something had to be done to put out the flames. When we opened the door to see where the other residents of the village were, we saw about fifteen club-wielding men standing outside our four houses. Seeing us, one of them quickly moved forward and threatened us loudly in an angry voice, "You dogs! Go back inside your houses. We'll kill you if you try to come out." Scared, we went back inside and quickly barred the door. The man's ferocity and the conditions that had prevailed during the day convinced the women and children inside the house that the situation was serious and they were trapped. They all started crying. The same kind of hue and cry rose from the other three houses. It's inconceivable that our neighbours wouldn't have heard all this lamentation and crying, but no one came to our rescue. After a while, fear muffled the cries but the sobbing continued. We couldn't even imagine what was going to happen to us. Every member of the household, both big and small, sat holding his breath, waiting for death. Just then someone knocked at the door so violently that we thought it would disintegrate and that the men outside would barge in and kill us. The same person who had threatened us earlier, moved forward and shouted, "All the men and women in the house, come out as you are, come out in the street. If you try to pick up anything, we'll kill you." So all of us came out into the street. Our neighbours have a son named Rafiq. Maybe about ten. He found the threats and rebukes of the man so frightening that he went up the stairs and hid on the roof instead of coming out. In the confusion, no one paid attention to whether or not he'd come out. The men forced out the residents of the other three houses the same way and then splashed kerosene, or perhaps petrol, on the houses and set fire to them. They kicked and punched us and told us to get lost. When the houses caught fire, Rafiq was standing at the parapet calling out to his father loudly and crying. The stairs had caught fire. His father ran to the fields at the back of the house and started begging him to jump down. Finally, Rafiq mustered enough courage to jump. He was safe but both of his legs broke. I only know about these two wounded ones; Lord knows how many more have been injured. My father took all of us to the house of his sister who is not an Ahmadi. No Ahmadi household in the village is safe any more. While we were on our way to Phuphi's house, we met Ghulam Ali and Amjad who were coming to our place to see Rehmat Ilahi. My father told Ghulam Ali that Rehmat Ilahi had gone to town to see Chaudhry Bashir sahib. At that, Ghulam Ali told me to take Amjad with me, go to Sultanpur and tell you what had happened here and also that he is bringing Amjad's mother to town on the cart. He wants you to make arrangements for her immediate treatment. Amjad and I were leery of walking the deserted paths at night, so we persuaded Zafar and Majeed to come with us. Their houses have been charred as well. Amjad passed through the whole village on his way and he said that the belongings of not a single Ahmadi house have been spared. And the isolated houses were completely burned.'

'Who identified the Ahmadi houses?'

'We don't know.'

'There was to be a curfew in Noor Nagar until 5 a.m. Rehmat Ilahi sahib told us that, when he left the village, armed police were patrolling the streets. Where were they when the rioters burned the belongings and set fire to the houses?'

'We don't know where they were. We didn't see any police.'

All this time Zafar and Majeed sat like scared cats, staring at Bashir Ahmad.

It was oppressively muggy during the night but a pleasant breeze started blowing by early morning. This is how the signs of the breaking of the heat and closeness appeared during the last days of August and then vanished. Ever since Ismail had come to Sultanpur he had remained single, except for the short time when Barkatay was alive. After her death, he had again lived alone. Loneliness weighed heavily on his nerves and the thought of an aimless life sometimes drove him to the brink of craziness. Often at night, regardless of what time it was, he would leave the house in an agitated state and wander aimlessly through the deserted streets and alleyways. Gradually, he overcame his disorder to a large extent and, rather than fighting it, made peace with it. He found solace in small things, such as listening to the radio, reading newspapers and magazines, working in the kitchen, or cleaning the house, and he began deriving a kind of pleasure and joy from them. Then one day, during this routine that lasted for months, a thought suddenly appeared from somewhere that loneliness was churning inside his heart like a furious black whirlpool and might pull him in at any moment. At other times he felt as though the whirlpool that had been relentlessly eroding the inner walls of his heart, might some day burst through its crust, leaving behind a shapeless and colourless substance, like a wet kite in the hands of a child—two sticks and a wilted, dripping, discoloured piece of paper.

He had finished reading the newspaper and was now watering and sharing in the joy of jasmine and raat ki rani plants gently swaying in the breeze. The month of August came every year, the same August in which his parents, sisters, brothers, all his relatives were slaughtered by the Sikhs for the crime of being Muslims. 'Did it help the murderers, or benefit the Sikh religion itself in any way? No. Did the Muslims and Islam suffer any loss? No, except that those thirty or thirty-five people lost their lives. Most of them would have died by now anyway. Barkatay and I escaped—she was spared because of her youth and gender, only to die later, grieving over those who had perished. And I, who saved himself by fleeing from the battlefield, am still alive to celebrate the anniversary of their deaths and my own cowardice—a cowardice on which even Barkatay had put her seal of disapproval and certified it. Many Augusts have come and gone, and on each day of this month I have seen how the sun and the monsoon moisture blend together to produce the same fierce smells in the soil, the crops, the houses, the trees and the growth along the riverbank that I had come to know in August 1947. The Beas used to be my river in those days, just as much as Gobindpur's. It no longer belongs to me, though it still belongs to Gobindpur.

Even the Ravi, of which it used to be a tributary, isn't ours any more. Perhaps this same fragrance, which also wafted from the growth along the banks of the Ravi, was just to console and comfort me, but the river and I both forget it as soon as the rainy season is over. The events of the past keep coming back to me in the order they happened, perhaps only to sadden or, even worse, to embarrass me.'

A fearless golden sunlight had stretched out on the outer wall of the courtyard. Ismail looked at his watch. It was close to seven. He made tea and warmed the water for his shave. He put both the tea and the shaving kit on the table in the courtyard, rolled up his bedding, and drank his tea sip by sip sitting on the bare cot. Then he looked carefully at his face in the mirror: 'It wasn't so bad in my youth, but now this dark wrinkled face has been taken over entirely by white ants. Whoever said that termites never attack ebony? If I didn't have to shave, I'd never look into the mirror. What's left to look at, anyway?'

As he was lathering his face, the stacks of complaints about his old age got folded up in his mind and sent to their appropriate compartment, to be opened again the very next day.

'If the religious strife and the sectarian riots that flared up later as a result of Partition, hadn't gotten in my way, I would have spent my life quite differently as a well-known prosperous lawyer in Gobindpur. I would have had my own clan, my family. I would have been the head of a small Muslim community and instituted many different projects for their betterment that would have been needed in today's world. But then, it's possible I might not have done any of those things; even there I might have run an ordinary drugstore or been unsuccessful as a lawyer. Perhaps I never had the ability to go very far. "If the ocean weren't an ocean, it would have been a desert." Anyway, this may be what it is, but by what right did the Sikhs uproot me from Gobindpur and fling me here, and slaughter, though innocent of any crime, every member of my family?' Moisture welled up in his eyes and he quickly caught it in his towel. If it had spilled out, it would have streaked the lather and spread it over his whole face.

'All his life, Guru Nanak, the founder of the Sikh religion, talked about peace and reconciliation, and preached love and affection among people. He strove to eliminate the high and low created by caste divisions and gave mankind a lesson in equality based on the bond of humanity. From Mahavira and Gautama Buddha to Guru Nanak Dev, every great reformer in India considered caste discrimination an insult to mankind and spurned it, but every time, the selfish nature of those who wanted to benefit from it gradually took over. Leave aside India, even in Pakistan, a purely Islamic country created by partitioning India, the remains of the caste system still exist to this day in some form or the other. Such is the force of the preaching of the family priests and Brahmins on people's minds. To preserve their authority and material advantages, they warn the simple folks about the heart-rending consequences that will result from disobeying them, and the frightened people are thus psyched up to continue the oppression proposed by their priests, throwing all the established verities overboard. This is what the priests did in the Europe of the Dark Ages too. There, to avenge themselves on their detractors and adversaries, and to demonstrate their control and authority over people, the priests dubbed them heretics, sorcerers and witches and had them burned alive at the stake. Whenever that happened, the darkness of the Dark Ages became darker still and its layers thicker and denser.

'Sultanpur is a town of one hundred and fifty thousand, and the total population of Ahmadis, including the children and seniors, cannot be more than a hundred. For the past fifteen days, this fistful of people, in full view of the hundred and fifty thousand, have been spending their days shuddering with fear. There isn't a moment of the day or night when the fear of death leaves their hearts. Is this huge population not able to see what's happening, or does it just not want to? Is deliberate ignorance a convenient way to escape the ire and fury of the other party, and avoid the pangs of conscience? The majority appears so content, as if every individual in town is perfectly happy and cheerful in his home and faces no danger at all. To this day I can't put out of my mind everything I went through during the riots of 1947. There are many others here, the same age as I am, who faced similar deadly incidents back then and haven't forgotten their experience. Don't they understand the Ahmadis' fear and disquietude? Why don't they? Have they forgotten the menace that stuck to their walls and doors? Have they forgotten the eyes of the women and children bursting from the pressure of countless questions? Can't they remember how they prayed for help from the Invisible World, yet no help arrived? Has that time been erased from their minds when every footstep bore ill will and every moving thing was an enemy? Will they not even move their little finger to save the lives of one hundred people from the jaws of death? To save themselves from destruction, the Ahmadis have banged their heads up against the government offices time and again, and received the same standard answer: Your complaints are just illusions. Can no one else see what the Ahmadis are seeing?'

Around nine, Ismail got ready and left the house. He locked the door and walked slowly into the street. There, some people stood facing west, quietly staring at the sky. He also looked towards the west and, like the others, was struck dumb. He was confused and worried, and his lips didn't move. About three or four blocks in the distance, clouds of smoke rose quickly, shot straight up, shifted a little to the east in the direction of the wind, and then spread over the entire sky.

'Has someone's house caught fire?' Ismail asked.

A young man answered, 'Baba-ji, the whole street of the Mirzais is on fire.'

At the time of Partition, when Ismail was desperately seeking some refuge in Amritsar, he had witnessed the Muslims' Katra Jaimal Singh trading district burning, very much like the conflagration in front of him today. The Hindus and Sikhs had set it on fire to punish the Muslims for partitioning the country. So, all the apprehensions which the officials had been treating as illusions for the past fifteen days had, as if to eradicate their doubts once and for all, become real and were now staring them in the face! But what difference did it make? Those who were destined to be looted, were looted.

'Is there anyone inside the houses?' Ismail asked.

'No, they sneaked out of the back doors into the fields before the fire started.'

'Who told you this?'

'I've just been to the street myself. There's a mob outside in the main bazaar. I heard some people say that before the street gate could be pulled down, all the residents had escaped. I went around the street to the fields in the back but saw no one there. Who knows where they've taken off to.'

'Did you hear who set the fire?'

'They say it's the work of students from theological schools here as well as outside, joined by some boys from the city. They had some special kind of powder with them. They drizzled it and the second they threw a matchstick into it, flames flared up. You can't see anything along the street. It looks like a clay oven for roasting corn.'

A bit ashamed, his head bent low, Ismail thought as he walked, 'How do you teach a person who has suffered himself and yet doesn't have any feeling for the troubles of others?' He left the street and turned into the main bazaar towards his store. It was half past nine, yet the shops were still closed. Usually the bazaar was in full swing by nine in this weather. Today, perhaps fear of the fire had kept the shopkeepers away. They must have thought that, given the circumstances, if the mob decided to plunder their stores there would be little they could do. Traders are usually more sensitive than other people regarding money matters. Ismail looked at the sky once again. The smoke was still rising with the same volume and speed. Suddenly he saw the chunky dull-looking Munawwar running towards him in his clumsy unwieldy way, followed by three club-wielding young men with two others. It looked as if Munawwar would fall down any minute. As the boy came near, Ismail stretched out his arm, stopped him and asked: 'What happened?'

'Hitting me, they hitting me . . .'

Ismail told him in a loud voice, 'Munawwar, Munawwar, I'm Baba. You're safe with me. Don't worry. No one can hurt you. Nothing's going to happen to you. Have courage.'

Soaking in perspiration and shaking profusely, Munawwar was finding it hard to breathe. Tears were streaming down. He felt a little less panicky after he finally recognized Ismail.

Coming out of his house with his mother and the other people, and going through the fields, Munawwar had been utterly sick of his imprisonment of the past few days. As soon as he reached the main road, he pulled himself free of his mother's arm and ran. Who had time at that moment to run after him and catch him? His mother wailed and lamented a lot, but no one bothered. Finally, she went after him herself. Even though she had lived in Sultanpur for ages, she had no knowledge of the streets, paths and roads. She might have known them if she had ever stepped out of the four walls of her house, but what could she do now? Driven by motherly love, crying inside her chador, she wandered through the unknown and unseen streets.

The three students with clubs were from out of town. Ismail knew the other two. One was Shaikh Sardar Ali's son Asghar, and the second his friend Nemat Khan. In the meantime, many other people also gathered at the scene and the crowd became thicker. In a loud and authoritative voice, Ismail asked, 'What do you want with him?'

'This fellow is a Mirzai,' one of the students answered, 'and the Mirzais are responsible for subverting Islam. So, this fellow deserves to be killed.'

Noticing their menacing expressions and ghastly looks, Ismail modulated the tone of his voice but kept its gravity, composure and confidence intact. 'You three do not know that this man that you are bent on killing is neither a Mirzai, nor a Muslim, nor anything else. Don't you see he has no intelligence to form any opinion or adopt any faith? His ability to know or memorize the basics of any religion is equal to zero. In killing him you will not be killing a Mirzai, but someone who has the mental capacity of a child less than five years old. You will be killing an innocent person for a crime he cannot commit. Your two companions, Asghar and Nemat, who have identified this person as a Mirzai and suggested killing him, are well aware of this fact about him. Aren't you, Nemat and Asghar? Speak up now.'

'You're right,' both said.

'All these people who have gathered here are residents of Sultanpur. Every one of them knows this boy. Ask anyone you like whether what I've told you is right or wrong.'

Ten or fifteen people in the crowd spoke up in unison, 'Yes, it's right.'

The five of them were feeling very small now. They lost their nerve in the face of a crowd of adversaries and had turned around to slink away from the scene when Ismail called out, 'Wait! Listen to one more thing before you leave. I'm addressing these students especially. This earth is the common possession of all mankind, and everyone believing in any faith has an equal right to live on it. If you care to take notice, the non-Muslims are far greater in number in the world than Muslims. If everyone starts thinking that anyone who does not have exactly the same faith as we do, or who is not like us, should be killed, then by tomorrow morning, not even one person will be left alive on earth. Learn to listen to the viewpoints of others and have the patience to understand them. Go now.'

Those who had come with the intent to murder were now finding it difficult to run away and avoided meeting the eyes of the onlookers. As he walked towards his store holding on to Munawwar's arm, Ismail was thinking: 'If they had killed Munawwar today, would Ahmadiyyat be finished? No. The Sikhs killed hundreds of thousands of Muslims in India and forced millions of others to migrate here. Did Islam come to an end? No. Even today there are hundreds of thousands of Muslims still living in East Punjab. Such conflicts have nothing to do with religion and everything to do with group psychology. A majority group, by virtue of being a majority, holds enormous power within itself. At some level, the mind is aware of this and, as a result, wants it to be acknowledged. A weapon is a powerful tool. You give it to a kid and he'll surely try to use it. If there is no control and discipline to go along with it, what is happening now will occur unavoidably. When the boys who had come out to murder saw that they had become a minority in an opposing crowd, they took to their heels. Had I listened to Bashir Ahmad's suggestion and come out yesterday to explain to the people in this very bazaar the real reason behind the rally, they would certainly have listened, and it's very likely the houses and the property of the Ahmadis would have been spared.'